This book is dedicated to my children. You do not yet know the pain I locked inside or the scars I carry. But one day, you will—and you will understand why I fought so hard to become more than my past.

Table of Contents

Introduction:

My name is Sam Knutson, and I am a survivor. My life has been shaped by abuse, trauma, heartache, and moments of profound defeat. Yet this is not where my story ends—it is where it begins. I do not pretend to have all the answers, nor do I presume to understand the full depth of anyone else's experience. What I do know is who I am, and the path I walked to become that person.

As a child, I loved to write, but I rarely had the freedom to express myself honestly or fully. Within these pages, you will encounter pieces of the emotions, experiences, and memories that defined those early years. You may find yourself wondering how I kept going, how I found a way forward, or how I made it out at all. I still ask myself those same questions.

I created this book to give myself space to speak—to annotate, to reflect, and to give voice to the weight I have carried in silence for far too long. Many people know only the version of me that I allow the world to see. Beneath that exterior lies someone shaped by a troubled past—someone who has endured, adapted, and learned to keep moving even while carrying a painful past.

This is my attempt to let them see the person behind the façade. To show the real me. To let them know, this is me, as I am.

Before You Enter

I didn't set out to write a book about trauma. I set out to share a collection of poems I have written; poems about my trauma and my survival. I couldn't keep the weight inside anymore. Because at 3am when sleep wouldn't come, when my mind replayed every failure and every fear, when the hypervigilance that kept me safe as a child now kept me prisoner as an adult—I had to put it somewhere. So I wrote.

What started as private endeavor became something else: an emotional outpouring. This outpouring helped me, though I'm not sure I ever will be "healed". I'm done pretending that's the goal— but I did survive. These poems are my attempt to capture what my childhood trauma has turned into as an adult. Of my mechanisms I developed to function when "functional" is the best I could hope for. The moment I stopped asking "when will I be normal?" and started asking "how can I survive being like this?"

This book exists because the gap between how I experience the world and how others perceive me is vast and mostly invisible. I look fine. I show up, I achieve, I attempt to maintain relationships, I smile at appropriate moments. And everyone assumes that means I'm okay. They don't see that I'm reading every room for danger, that I'm running constant threat assessments, that I'm exhausted from the performance of seeming fine. They don't see the hypervigilance, the catastrophizing, the inability to trust, the oscillation between numbness and overwhelming feeling—all the internal machinery that trauma installed and that won't shut off even when I'm safe.

So I wrote it down. The symptoms first, because that's what I experienced first—the relationship struggles, the emotional dysregulation, the constant planning that stole any possibility of joy. Then the survival strategies, the ways I learned to carry invisible weight while appearing strong, the fortress I built from my own damage. And finally, the source—my house of wrath, my fallen beacon, the specific abuse that created all these patterns within me.

Who This Book Is For

Me.

That's the honest answer. After years of repressing my trauma, I found an outlet and I needed to get my words down. I didn't write this to help anyone. I wrote it to survive. To stop the 3am replays. To give the demons names so they'd stop whispering in the dark.

But.

If you read this and you connect with what I'm saying—if you see yourself in the hypervigilance, the emotional numbness, the exhaustion of performing "fine"—then this book is for you too.

I don't claim to know the first thing about your trauma. I only know mine because I lived through it, and I still feel the effects every day. Your pain is your own. Your story is different. But maybe the shape is similar. Maybe the mechanisms match. Maybe darkness recognizes darkness, and there's something valuable in that recognition.

If you're reading this because someone you love is struggling, maybe these poems can give you language for what they can't articulate. Maybe you'll understand why they test you, why they plan everything obsessively, why they seem fine one moment and unreachable the next. One of the main themes across all three collections is that we all wear masks and pretend we're okay. But underneath? We're all broken in different ways, and maybe that brokenness is what connects us.

So this book is for me. But if you need it, it's for you too.

Why Three Collections in This Order

I structured this book backward from how I lived it. You'll see the effects before you see the cause.

That's intentional. Because that's how trauma actually works—you experience the symptoms for years, sometimes decades, before you understand their source.

Collection I: What I Feel Inside documents the struggle from inside. The inability to trust, the hypervigilance, the emotional flatness punctuated by overwhelming feeling, the yearning for connection alongside the terror of it. These poems reach tentatively toward others, hoping that connection might heal what I couldn't name yet.

Collection II: The Weight of Me is colder. Harder. It's what happened when I realized nobody else could carry this weight—I had to do it alone. These poems document achievement that nobody sees, the exhaustion of appearing fine, the horror of recognizing your abuser in your own reflection. They end with a declaration: survival itself is victory, even when it's ugly.

Collection III: My Demons descends into the source. Here I stop speaking in symptoms and start naming what caused them. This is where it gets specific. Where I stop protecting anyone—including myself. This collection goes to places I spent years trying to keep buried.

Reading them in this order, you'll experience what I experienced: symptoms before understanding, effects before cause, the slow realization of why I am the way I am. Each collection recontextualizes the ones before it.

By the time you reach Collection III, you'll understand why Collections I and II had to exist first. You'll see how the foundation cracks, and everything built on top of it cracks too.

About the Summaries

You'll notice each poem is followed by a summary—a "codex" that unpacks what's really happening beneath the metaphors. I included these because the poems operate on two levels. Read without context, they're about universal struggles with trust, control, identity. Read with context, they're specific documentation of how severe trauma rewires human psychology.

The summaries aren't literary analysis. They're me, holding your hand, saying "here's what was actually happening when I wrote this." They're intimate companion rather than academic guide. I want you to read the poem first, form your own response, then gain the deeper context. Some of you will flip back and forth constantly. Some will read all the poems first, then return for the summaries. Some will want the context before encountering the piece. However you use them is right.

What You Need to Know Before Starting

This book deals with heavy emotional content. I write about the effects of childhood trauma—hypervigilance, trust issues, emotional numbness, relationship struggles. Collection III gets more specific about the sources: an abusive father, an absent mother, toxic relationships. But I'm not writing graphic descriptions of abuse. I'm writing about what living with those experiences did to me, how they shaped the way I move through the world.

Some of this might resonate uncomfortably if you've experienced similar things. If something hits too hard:

You can stop. Put the book down. Come back when you're ready, or don't. There's no obligation to finish.

You can skip pieces. The summaries tell you what's coming. If a topic feels like too much, skip it. Each poem stands alone.

You can take your time. Read one piece and sit with it. This isn't meant to be consumed in one sitting.

But honestly? Most of this is probably stuff you've felt if you're reading a book about trauma. The hypervigilance. The exhaustion of seeming fine. The wondering if you'll ever feel normal. The questioning whether anyone would stay if they really knew you.

If that's you, you'll recognize yourself here. And maybe that recognition helps. Maybe it just hurts. Both are okay.

What This Book Isn't

This isn't a redemption story. My abusers don't get their comeuppance. There's no justice, no transformation, no moment where they realize what they did and apologize. That's not how it worked for me.

This isn't about forgiveness. I haven't forgotten and I'm not easy to forgive.

This isn't about transcendence. I haven't risen above my trauma into some enlightened state. I haven't turned my pain into wisdom. I'm just trying to function.

This isn't a healing journey. I'm managing, not healed. Some days are better than others. Some days I'm still that kid reading danger in floorboard creaks. That's my reality.

This isn't inspiration. I'm not going to tell you "it gets better" because sometimes it doesn't get better—it gets managed. You get stronger, or at least more practiced at carrying the weight. But "better" suggests less damaged, and for me, I'm still damaged but better managed.

What This Book Is:

Honest. About my trauma, how it feels, what survival costs me. No sugar-coating, no tidy narrative arc.

Specific. If you've experienced something similar, you might see yourself in me. The hypervigilance, the relationship struggles, the exhaustion of performing "fine"—it's all documented with the kind of detail that only comes from living it.

Company, maybe. If you're carrying similar weight, at least you'll know someone else has carried it too. Every shameful, exhausting detail—you're not the only one.

Permission. To manage instead of heal. You have my permission, even though in the end it doesn't matter, to just manage the burden to the best of your ability. To survive instead of thrive. To be a work-in-progress indefinitely. You don't have to be "fixed" to be worthy of your life.

One person's map. Not prescriptive—your path is different than mine—but descriptive. This is what it looked like for me to survive what I survived. Maybe some of it is useful. Maybe none of it is. Either way, it's real.

What I Believe About Healing Now

I used to think healing meant going back to who I was before all this happened. Then I realized—there is no "before." The trauma started when I was a kid, while I was still being formed. The person I might have been without it never got a chance to exist.

So healing can't mean restoration. For me, it means something simpler: control. Not control over what happened—that's gone. Not control over the permanent effects—those are woven in. But control over how I respond to them now. Whether I let the bad days consume me or whether I manage them. Whether my trauma runs me or whether I run it.

I still have bad days. Days where I'm hypervigilant for no reason. Days where I can't trust anyone. Days where I see my father in the mirror and hate myself for it. But more and more, I get to decide what I do with those days instead of them deciding for me.

That's not the ending anyone would choose. It's not inspiring. But it's real, and it's mine.

What I Need You to Understand

I wrote this for me. To get the weight out of my head and onto paper where I could see it.

But now it exists, and you're reading it, so here's what I want you to know:

I'm not your spokesperson. I don't speak for trauma survivors as a group. I speak for myself. My trauma, my mechanisms, my survival. If you see yourself in this, that's between you and the page.

I'm not your guide. I don't have answers for you. I barely have answers for myself. Some days I manage. Some days I don't. That's just how it is.

I'm not fixed. Writing this didn't heal me. Publishing this won't heal me. I'm still hypervigilant. I still see my father in the mirror sometimes. I still have days where trust feels impossible. This book is documentation, not triumph.

I'm not easy. The people in my life will tell you that. I test relationships. I plan obsessively. I keep distance even when I don't want to. That's what this trauma made me. I'm working on it, but I'm not promising to change.

I'm not asking for pity. I survived. I'm still here. That's enough for me.

If you're reading this because you love someone with trauma—good. Maybe this helps you understand them. Maybe it doesn't. Either way, your patience matters more than you know.

If you're reading this because you're curious about trauma—now you know what it looks like from the inside. It's uglier and more mundane than you probably expected.

What Scares Me About This

I'm not scared my family will read this. I'm scared of how they'll react when they do.

We don't talk about feelings in my family. It makes people uncomfortable. It's easier to keep things surface-level, to pretend the past is the past and doesn't need examining. But I can't do that anymore. This book exists because I needed to examine it. I needed to put words to experiences that have shaped every part of who I am.

We all experienced the same events, but we experienced them from different perspectives. That's just reality. My father lived through his childhood. My mother lived through hers. My brothers had their experiences. And I had mine. None of those perspectives cancel out the others. They all existed simultaneously, even when they contradict each other.

This is how I interpreted what happened. How I felt living through it. The fear I carried. The hypervigilance I developed. The ways I learned to read danger in sounds and silences. That was my reality as a kid, regardless of what anyone else's reality was.

If they remember it differently—if my father thinks he was just maintaining discipline, if my mother thinks she was doing her best, if anyone thinks I'm exaggerating or misremembering—that's their perspective. They're entitled to it. But they can't take away how I felt. They can't tell me my experience wasn't real just because it doesn't match their memory or their intent.

Intent doesn't erase impact. What they meant to do doesn't change what actually happened to me.

I'm not asking their permission to write this. I'm not running it by them for approval. I'm not softening it to make them more comfortable. This is the way I experienced it.

And I want to be clear: I'm not speaking poorly about who they are today. People change. People grow. The person my mother is now isn't necessarily the person she was when I was seven, or twelve, or sixteen. This book isn't an indictment of who my family has become. It's documentation of what I lived through and how it affected me.

I'm writing about how I felt as a kid going through what I went through. The terror. The confusion. The desperate attempt to understand why things were the way they were. That kid deserves to have his experience acknowledged, even if it makes the adults uncomfortable now.

I'm not that kid anymore. I'm a grown man. I've spent decades processing this, managing it, learning to function despite it. I'm writing from that adult perspective, with adult understanding, but I'm writing about childhood experience. About the foundation that was laid before I had any say in it.

This is my story to tell. Not theirs to approve. Not theirs to edit. Not theirs to deny.

Mine.

How to Read This Book

However you want.

All at once or spread out over months. In order or skipping around to whatever pieces call to you. Alone or with someone you trust nearby. Taking notes in the margins or keeping it clean. Crying, or numb, or pissed off, or cycling through all three.

There's no right way to do this.

When you're ready, start with Collection I. That's where I started— inside the struggle, not understanding where it came from yet, reaching for connection I wasn't sure I could trust.

It goes deeper from there.

Collection I

What I Feel Inside

This is the collection about the gap—the distance between what you show and what you carry. About performing "fine" so convincingly that even you start to believe it. About the weight that's invisible to everyone else, the pain you've learned to hide so well it became your default setting. This is about living in that space between who you appear to be and who you actually are, and forgetting which version is real.

What This Collection Is

This is about the split—the me that exists in public versus the me that exists in private. The mask isn't always intentional; sometimes I've worn it so long I can't remember putting it on. These poems document what happens in the space between the performance and the truth, between the face I show and the storm I hide.

This collection lives in my internal world—the thoughts I don't voice, the feelings I've learned to bury, the truth that only comes out at 3am when I can't sleep. It's about emotional isolation even when I'm surrounded by people, about the exhaustion of maintaining a facade, about wondering if anyone would stay if they saw what I actually carry.

It opens in the wreckage of broken trust and moves through the various survival strategies that trauma produces. The journey goes from damage to compensation to consequence, through the mechanisms I developed to cope, and concludes with a fragile but deliberate reach toward connection—tentative, uncertain, but real.

Key Themes

The Paradox of Self-Protection: Every defensive strategy I employ to avoid pain ultimately creates new forms of suffering. Emotional guardedness prevents hurt but also blocks intimacy. Hyper-planning provides control but eliminates joy. Silence avoids vulnerability but ensures misunderstanding. Speaking up risks rejection but taints every response with doubt. These were survival strategies once. Now they are my prison.

The Trap of Hypervigilance: I exist in a state of exhausting alertness—remembering everything, analyzing every interaction, searching for warning signs, preparing for inevitable abandonment. This constant surveillance stems from past betrayals but prevents present peace. My mind is both protector and tormentor, unable to distinguish between genuine threat and benign moment.

The Cost on Present Relationships: Past wounds don't stay in the past—they actively distort current reality. My marriage suffers not from any present failure but from ghosts of previous relationships. Every kindness gets filtered through suspicion, every silence interpreted as withdrawal, every moment of peace treated as the calm before abandonment. Unhealed trauma doesn't just affect me—it impacts everyone trying to love me.

The Oscillation Between Extremes: I experience emotional life as binary switches rather than spectrums—feeling too much or nothing at all, planning everything or drowning in chaos, believing I'm worthless or tentatively grasping at self-worth. There's little stable middle ground. My nervous system is dysregulated by trauma and operating in persistent survival mode.

Memory as Both Gift and Curse: I remember in vivid detail. I analyze deeply. I notice patterns. These capacities could be strengths but they've become instruments of self-torture. My mind replays past conversations endlessly, constructs elaborate interpretations from minimal data, and uses its considerable analytical power to build cases for unworthiness or impending disaster.

The Loneliness of Internal Experience: A profound isolation runs through this collection—the sense that these struggles are uniquely shameful, that everyone else navigates life with ease while I battle invisible demons. The mask captures how performing normalcy prevents genuine connection, creating a feedback loop where hiding pain ensures continued isolation.

The Possibility of Shared Humanity: The collection's most significant shift comes in recognizing that these intense personal struggles might be universal human experiences rather than individual failures. That others also mask pain, also fear abandonment, also question their worth. This realization transforms isolation into potential community.

Why I Wrote This

I wrote these poems in the space between my public self and my private self. The version of me that goes to work, shows up for people, handles responsibilities—that version is real. But so is the version that stares at walls at 3am wondering what the point is. So is the version that feels nothing and chases anything that might make me feel something. So is the version that's so tired of holding it together that even breathing feels like labor.

What scared me most wasn't the pain—it was the numbness. Pain at least confirms you're alive. Numbness is different. It's watching my life happen to someone else. It's knowing objectively that things should matter but feeling nothing where the mattering should be.

These poems are what I couldn't say out loud because saying it would mean admitting I wasn't okay, and I'd built my entire identity around being the one who handles things, who doesn't break, who doesn't need help.

The Emotional Journey

This collection operates primarily in registers of anxiety, doubt, and exhaustion. There's persistent fear threading through nearly every piece—fear of abandonment, of inadequacy, of losing control, of feeling too much or not at all. This anxiety produces a bone-deep weariness. I'm tired of hypervigilance, tired of analysis, tired of self-protection, yet unable to stop these automatic patterns.

The apathy appears not as peaceful acceptance but as traumatic shutdown—the system overwhelmed into numbness. Yet beneath this flatness runs desperate longing: for trust, for joy, for presence, for connection, for the ability to simply receive love without dissecting it.

The emotional tone shifts in the final pieces toward something more tender—not resolution exactly, but vulnerability. I stop trying to fix myself and instead offer my brokenness as the basis for connection.

The Arc

Where it starts: Behind the mask. The performance is working. Nobody sees the storm.

Where it moves: Through compensation—hyperplanning, silent expectations, questioning every gesture of care. Through consequence—the constant fear of not being enough, the numbness that comes from feeling too much.

Where it questions: The mechanisms I've built—the obsessive memory, the catastrophic interpretations, the oscillation between worthlessness and tentative self-belief. Is there a real self underneath all this? Or have I become nothing but reactions and compensations?

Where it arrives: Recognition. Behind the mask. The realization that maybe everyone is struggling, maybe these battles aren't uniquely mine, maybe connection is possible if I'm willing to be seen as broken.

Where it ends: With an invitation. Tentative, fragile, but deliberate. A reach toward authentic human connection. The suggestion that maybe we can be broken together, and in that togetherness, find something resembling freedom.

This collection doesn't resolve. It doesn't claim I've overcome anything. It documents the struggle and ends with a question: if you feel this too, you're not alone. Maybe that recognition is enough. Maybe connection—real, vulnerable, mutual recognition of shared struggle—might offer what individual willpower cannot.

Content Warning

This collection deals with emotional numbness, depression, anxiety that goes unwitnessed, suicidal ideation, the exhaustion of performing functionality, and the question of whether a self exists beneath the survival strategies. The tone shifts between hollow calm and desperate internal screaming—the flat effect of someone who's learned that showing pain makes things worse.

I Couldn't See

Every bond I built had cracks I couldn't see,
Smiles that faded once they got what they need.
Now I trace the lines where love used to be,
And wonder if it ever was for me.
I've learned to flinch before I fall,
Expect goodbye before the call.
It's safer not to trust too deep—
At least the hurt don't cut as steep.

Every hand that swore they'd stay,
Turned their back or slipped away.
Parents said they cared, but left me guessing,
Friends turned truth into a weapon.
I gave pieces till I was hollow,
Learned love means debt you can't swallow.
Now I guard what's left inside,
Smile soft, but never wide.

They tell me, "Open up, it's fine."
But I've seen what waits behind that line.
Promises sound sweet in spring,
But I've lived through what the winters bring.
I've been taught that warmth's a phase,
That comfort always decays.
So I built my walls from calm replies,
Numb control behind tired eyes.

I want to give my heart and mean it,
But I don't trust that they'll keep it.
I test their tone, I read each word,
Trying to catch the shift before it's heard.
My partner says I'm distant, cold,
But this is how I've learned to hold—
Enough to show that I still care,
But never more than I can spare.

I don't hate the ones who broke me,
They just wrote the code that runs me.

I can't rewrite it overnight,
But I'm trying hard to make it right.
Every scar a quiet guide,
Every ghost still walks beside.
I trace them all but keep on breathing,
Broken faith, but still believing.

I want to love without defense,
To trust without pretense.
To stop waiting for the end,
Every time I find a friend.
But I'm scared of peace I can't control,
Scared of hands that might let go.
I tell myself I've made it through —
But I never stopped looking for proof.

Still, there's hope beneath the doubt,
A softer voice that whispers out.
Maybe love's not meant to be earned,
But something you relearn.
And maybe all this pain I keep,
Is just a seed beneath the grief.
One day, if I let it grow,
Maybe I'll finally let them know.

Every bond I built had cracks I couldn't see,
But maybe that's what made me — me.
And if I ever trust again,
It'll be because I chose to begin.
I can't erase what they took from me,
But I can choose what I let be.
Every scar still sings inside,
Proof I lived, and I survived.
I'm learning that love don't need to prove,
It just asks you not to move.
And maybe someday, if I believe,
It won't be so hard to receive.

Song Summary:
The painful realization that I missed critical red flags in a relationship because I was too invested in what I wanted it to be.

What I Was Actually Writing About:
There have been several instances in my life where I had friends who were not truly my friends. I had relationships where the woman I was dating was manipulative. I couldn't see the red flags and it ended up hurting me a lot. Every significant relationship that fell apart—romantic partners, friends, family—people who said they'd stay but didn't. The "cracks I couldn't see" weren't just metaphor. I genuinely couldn't recognize the warning signs. Or maybe I could, but I didn't want to. Each time someone promised permanence and then left, I learned the same lesson: connection is conditional. People leave.

The Pattern/Mechanism:
So I developed a defensive posture. I learned to anticipate abandonment instead of trusting stability. My parents left me guessing—never quite sure where I stood, what I'd done wrong, whether their care was real or conditional. Friends weaponized truth—used what I'd shared in vulnerability against me later. Romantic partners eventually withdrew, even the ones who swore they wouldn't. All of that collectively shaped how I approach relationships now. Emotional investment feels inherently risky. So I offer measured affection—never more than I can afford to lose. I maintain emotional distance. I test people constantly, looking for proof they'll stay or confirmation they'll leave.

The Tension:
There's internal conflict here—the desire for authentic connection fighting against the deeply ingrained fear of being hurt again. I know these defensive patterns were necessary for survival once. I also know they're limiting the possibility of genuine intimacy now. I want to trust that someone will stay, but every past experience has taught me they won't. So I keep one foot always ready to run, always prepared for the inevitable moment when they realize I'm not worth staying for.

Where I Am With This:

The closing verses introduce tentative hope. Not certainty, not transformation—just the possibility that trust might be something I can relearn rather than something permanently lost. That choosing vulnerability could be an act of agency rather than naiveté. This is the tension I'm living in: self-preservation versus the human need for connection. Past wounds shaping present relationships. The question of whether healing is even possible, or if the best I can do is choose vulnerability despite the scars.

Satisfied, Not Happy

Every day I plot my next move, one step at a time.
They say I should stop and breathe, but I can't quiet my mind.
My peace comes in plans, not in sunsets.
I don't chase joy—I chase what comes next.
Every win feels like relief, not light.
Every smile feels staged and tight.
Maybe that's just who I became,
Chasing order inside my brain.

I plan my future like a blueprint,
No rest, no guess—just movement.
Peace is numbers, stats, and scores,
Every calm moment feels like chores.
I measure life in completed goals,
Not in laughter or letting go.
I'm addicted to control, not pride—
Just the silence after the storm subsides.
I don't dance, I diagram steps,
Don't relax, I analyze depth.
They call it focus, I call it fear,
'Cause stillness means my thoughts get near.
My heart don't trust a quiet room,
It plans escape before it blooms.
I stay sharp when the lights are low,
'Cause peace don't mean control, you know.

I tell myself it's purpose, not prison,
But the walls feel closer every decision.
I built a kingdom made of plans,
But I forgot to use my hands.

I don't feel joy, I feel completion,
A quiet calm from a planned precision.
My heart don't sing, it calculates,
Every smile feels like a fake escape.
I want to stop, but I'm terrified,
That peace means losing what kept me alive.
So I stand here—calm but cold,

Satisfied, but never whole.

I chase order like oxygen,
Chaos knocks, I don't let it in.
They talk joy, I talk design,
I see paths, they see time.
I've been trapped by what I master,
Built a cage of "better" faster.
Balance feels like losing ground,
Every pause lets the doubt surround.
I crave comfort, but I stall,
Can't risk feeling, can't risk fall.
Every plan's a safety net,
Every breath's a calculated bet.
I want joy but it feels too raw,
Like fire under skin, no law.
I'm alive, but just controlled,
I built a world that won't unfold.

What if I could breathe without a reason?
What if joy wasn't weakness, but freedom?
What if peace don't need a plan —
Just a heart and an open hand?
Maybe one day, I'll try to see,
That peace was always chasing me.

I don't feel joy, I feel completion,
But I'm tired of this cold precision.
My heart wants noise, not just design,
A spark that breaks this ordered line.
Maybe peace is found in scars,
Not in maps or measured parts.
I built a world that feels controlled —
But I'm still searching for my soul.

I'm learning that satisfaction isn't the same as joy.
One keeps me moving…
The other might let me live.
Maybe someday — I'll choose both.

Song Summary:
The exhausting strategy of perpetually planning every scenario three to four moves ahead, where good outcomes bring validation instead of joy and nothing ever feels surprising anymore.

What I Was Actually Writing About:
With all the trauma in my life I've subconsciously planned for every scenario. I think about what will happen if I do something. This isn't uncommon—it's cause and effect—but I do it at such an unhealthy level that I'm planning three to four moves ahead, thinking about every possible scenario, good or bad. I plan out every situation in my head. I know every likely result before it happens. I weigh outcomes and hedge my bets. I run simulations of conversations, events, scenarios—mapping all the branches, anticipating the variables. By the time something actually occurs, I've already experienced multiple versions of it mentally. Because of this I no longer feel joy when something good does happen. I feel validation because my plans went according to plan. When things don't go my way I feel disappointment, and the need to recalibrate my internal algorithms. Hence, I feel satisfied, not happy.

The Pattern/Mechanism:
This might sound strategic. Maybe even smart. But here's what it costs: I'm never happy. I'm just satisfied with the outcome when it matches my prediction, or disappointed when I got something wrong. There's no joy in things going well because I already knew they would. There's no relief in dodging disaster because I'd already planned around it. Life becomes a series of confirmed predictions rather than lived experiences. The distinction between satisfaction and happiness is the core. Satisfaction is the absence of chaos—a successfully executed plan. Happiness is something else entirely. It's spontaneous. It requires not knowing what comes next. It requires being present in the moment rather than three steps ahead. And that terrifies me.

The Tension:
Maybe this stems from my trauma as a child. Maybe it's how my brain learned to create safety in an unsafe environment—by becoming a prediction machine, by never being surprised, by always

36

staying ahead of the chaos. But that skill doesn't turn off when you're safe. Peace without a plan feels like standing at the edge of a cliff. Spontaneity feels reckless. Joy without preparation feels dangerous. So I keep planning, keep predicting, keep staying three moves ahead. And I feel satisfied when I'm right. But I never feel happy.

Where I Am With This:

So I chase satisfaction instead. The relief of a completed checklist. The calm of having anticipated every variable. The validation when my prediction was correct. It's not happiness, but it's controllable. And control feels safer than joy. This is what the jouskas and over-planning anxiety look like from the inside. It's about using prediction as armor. It's about trading the possibility of joy for the certainty of not being blindsided. I know how things will go before they happen. And when they go that way, I feel... nothing. Just confirmation. And when I'm wrong? That's not just disappointment. It's destabilization. It's proof that my control was illusory. And surprise feels like threat.

Silent Expectations

I built my world on what I didn't say,
Thinking silence would make them stay.
Every plan looked clean in my head,
Till I watched it fall apart instead.
They never knew what I needed done,
I thought they'd just see where I was from.
Now I stare at the wreck I made,
All from words I was too afraid to trade.

I script my dreams like perfect plays,
But choke the lines when it's time to say.
I blame the world for missing cues,
But I'm the one who hides the truth.
Keep my wants locked deep inside,
Then curse the dark when they don't align.
I build blueprints made of pride,
Then drown in the quiet I designed.
Every time I wait too long,
The silence twists and proves me wrong.
They move on while I rehearse,
Rewrite the words that make it worse.
I see the cracks, I see the cost,
All the things I never lost—
'Cause I never had the nerve to show,
What I wanted them to know.

I don't say it, I just stare,
Hoping someone feels it there.
But no one hears what I don't tell—
I built this quiet, it's my shell.

I wanted more but never spoke,
Now I'm choking on my own hope.
I plan perfection, breathe regret,
Every silence leaves a debt.
I hold back till the moment's gone,
Then ask why no one heard my song.
I wanted love, but played pretend—

Silent expectations never end.

They say "communication's key,"
But I lock the door and swallow the key.
I want connection, not control,
But silence feels like self-control.
So I test them, wait, and watch,
Count their words like ticking clocks.
When they fail, I nod and grin—
Pretend I knew it from within.
I hate the loop, but never stop,
Push them close, then let them drop.
Every heartbreak feels rehearsed,
Like I planned the ending first.
They don't know what I didn't share,
They only saw me standing there.
Now I see the proof so clear—
My silence built this atmosphere.

What if I just said what I meant?
Would the walls still be this bent?
I wanted peace, I built control,
But silence cost me something whole.
Now the echoes all sound the same—
Every "almost" bears my name.
I wanted more but never spoke,
Now I'm haunted by the words I choked.

I built my calm, but it became the end,
Silent expectations never bend.
I crave the truth, but bite my tongue,
Pretend I'm fine, then come undone.
All this quiet feels like blame—
I'm the silence I became.

Maybe next time I'll just say it plain,
Before the silence starts again.
Till then, I'll sit inside my head—
Speaking to ghosts instead.

Song Summary:

The pattern of suppressing my own needs while resenting others for not magically knowing what I want but never voiced.

What I Was Actually Writing About:

Because of my hyper planning I tend to think that other people are capable of doing the same thing as me. And with that hyper-planning, I expect people to pick up on the subtle cues like I do. I think that people should know what I'm thinking because I've laid an intricate trail of breadcrumbs that I see as clear and obvious. I operate under the assumption that hints and behaviors should be sufficient—that if someone really cares, they'll intuitively understand what I need without me having to say it explicitly. Plans look clean in my head. Perfect, actually. Then I watch them fall apart because I never shared them with anyone else. They were supposed to just know. I know people cannot read my mind, but when I'm capable of picking up on hints and seeing patterns, I believe others should be able to as well. This has caused some issues with my wife as I feel like she should know but she doesn't.

The Pattern/Mechanism:

The central conflict is between internal clarity and external silence. Inside my head, everything is obvious. What I want, what I need, how things should go. But I don't say any of it out loud. Then I get frustrated when things don't happen the way I planned. I blame others for missing cues while I'm actively hiding the truth. I build resentment over needs I never actually voiced. I script dreams like perfect plays. I rehearse conversations. I plan exactly what I want to happen. But when it's time to actually speak? I choke. Then I curse the darkness of misunderstanding that I created.

The Tension:

Communication feels vulnerable. It feels like relinquishing control. If I have to ask for something directly, then I can't know if they're doing it because they want to or because I asked. So instead, I test relationships through silence. I wait to see if they'll prove their care by reading my mind. When they inevitably fail this impossible test, it becomes evidence. See? They don't really care. They don't really know me. It confirms the pre-existing doubt instead of revealing what it actually is — a communication breakdown that I caused.

Where I Am With This:

I see the cracks. I see the cost. My relationships suffer because I refuse to just say what I mean. People who care about me are left guessing, trying to decode behaviors and hints, inevitably getting it wrong because nobody can read minds. But recognizing the pattern and breaking it are different things. The closing lines acknowledge that silence has become both shield and prison. It protects me from the vulnerability of direct communication, but it also ensures I stay isolated, misunderstood, resentful. There's a glimmer of intention toward change — "Maybe next time I'll just say it plain." But the final image is "speaking to ghosts instead." I'm still rehearsing conversations internally rather than risking authentic, direct communication. The pattern persists because as much as silence hurts, vulnerability feels more dangerous.

Only Because I Said

Every gesture feels like an echo of me,
A shadow of what I asked, not what I see.
I know you care, I feel your hand,
But still I doubt, can't understand.
Every word I speak seems to bend the tide,
And I wonder if love can exist outside.
I want to trust, I want to believe,

I tell you what I need, you make it real,
But I ask—was it love, or just my will?
I see your eyes, I feel your care,
Still I question if you'd act if I wasn't there.
I crave your warmth, but fear the plan,
That I command affection more than I am.
Every smile, every hug, every small attempt,
Feels like an answer to the words I've sent.
I know your heart is there for me,
I see the proof in what you do and say.
But my mind rewinds every scene,
And I wonder if it would happen another way.
I want to rest, let the doubt fall through,
But I can't escape the "only because I said so" view.
Love feels heavy when trust is thin,
A constant war I cannot win.

I want to believe it's not a chore,
That your love exists outside my request, more.
I test each tone, I read each move,
Hoping to find the proof of your true groove.
It's hard to let the heart relax,
I wish I could just feel your care,
Without the shadow of doubt always there.

I know you love me, I feel it in part,
But there's a whisper that pulls at my heart.
Every kindness seems a response to my say,
And I can't shake the grief that it's not that way.
I want to trust, I want to let it be,

To feel your love exist independently.
Every proof is clouded by my mind,
Seeking truth that's hard to find.

I see the care in what you do,
But doubt still colors every hue.
I wish I could stop overthinking,
Stop counting moves like I'm linking.
Each gesture, each word, each small display,
Feels like a token to my say.
I long to rest in love's pure state,
Not in the echo of what I dictate.
Still, I feel the love that you provide,
Even when suspicion sits beside.
Maybe one day, I'll let it go,
And just accept what your heart shows.
But until then, I wrestle with grief,
Hoping trust will bring relief.
I want to love without the check,
To feel the care, not just the effect.

What if your love exists without my call?
What if you care beyond my wall?
Can I let go of proof and plan,
And just feel the love, as it began?
Maybe one day, I'll finally see,
Your heart beats freely, not for me.

I know you love me, I feel it true,
But the doubt still shadows what I view.
Every act a question in my mind,
Yet I long to leave the fear behind.
I want to trust that love is whole,
That your care exists beyond my role.
Every proof may never ease,
But I'm trying to believe in what I see.

Maybe one day I'll let it rest,
Feel your love without the test.
Until then, I'll breathe, I'll try,
To see your care beyond my eye.

Song Summary:
The exhausting need to explicitly state every desire because I can't trust that anyone will anticipate my needs or care without being told.

What I Was Actually Writing About:
This song is the opposite of Silent Expectations because in this one I actually do voice my opinion but then I feel like people only do things because I said it. You just read the sequel to "Silent Expectations." In that song, I stayed silent and resented people for not reading my mind. In this one, I finally spoke up—and now I can't trust any response I get. Here's the paradoxical trap: Having tried to articulate my needs, I now question whether every response is genuine affection or mere compliance. Did they do this because they wanted to, or only because I asked? When I make a meal, when I write a song, when I do anything, I ask if they like it and I feel like they say yes only because I asked the question, not because they actually like it. I believe that people are so afraid of confrontation that they will say something nice because saying something critical will cause strife. I know I've said people's cooking was good enough though it was in desperate need of salt, so other people do it as well.

The Pattern/Mechanism:
Every gesture feels like an echo of me. A shadow of what I requested, not what I actually see. I recognize my partner's efforts. I feel the care being offered. But I can't escape the interpretation that love expressed after being requested is somehow less authentic than love offered spontaneously. This creates a painful double bind. Silence leads to unmet needs—I learned that the hard way. But speaking up taints every subsequent action with doubt. If I have to ask for something, how do I know they wouldn't have done it anyway? How do I know it's real? My partner does something kind. My immediate thought: "Is this because they want to, or because I told them I needed it?" I constantly rewind every scene, analyzing whether the kindness would have occurred organically or only materialized because I explicitly named it.

The Tension:
This hypervigilance transforms relationship dynamics into something transactional. Every act of affection carries the weight of

uncertainty rather than providing comfort. I'm keeping a mental ledger: spontaneous gesture or response to request? Real care or obligation? Despite intellectual acknowledgment, emotional conviction remains elusive. I'm caught in exhausting mental loops. I can't simply receive love without dissecting its origins. Where did this come from? Would this have happened if I hadn't said anything? Am I experiencing genuine affection or just witnessing the results of my own direction?

Where I Am With This:

Maybe one day I'll trust that my partner's care and affection exists independently of instruction. That they would do these things even if I never asked. But until then, I remain trapped in analysis. Forever questioning. Forever doubting. Unable to just accept care at face value because I'm terrified it's performative, obligatory, a response to my request rather than a genuine impulse. This is what happens when you experience countless flawed relationships, you learn that love is conditional, that care has to be earned, that people only give what they're required to give. Even when someone loves you freely, you can't believe it. You dissect every gesture, looking for the strings attached. And if you had to ask for it? Then it definitely doesn't count.

Am I Enough

I gave my all, but the shadows stayed,
Every bond I built slowly frayed.
The life I made keeps testing me,
A mirror of what I can't let be.

I bleed effort but feel the void,
Every heart I touched got destroyed.
Even love I hold in my hands,
Feels like sand slipping through demands.
I plan, I care, I sacrifice,
But somehow I don't meet the price.
Every whisper of doubt I feel,
Shadows remind me nothing's real.
I see their eyes, searching for me,
But all I sense is uncertainty.
I want to believe, I try to trust,
But fear turns warmth into dust.
Maybe I'm broken, maybe I'm flawed,
Or maybe life just isn't awed.
Each day I fight to stand my ground,
Yet past shadows always surround.

I want to know I'm enough,
But silence makes it tough.
Even when they say they care,
I feel the weight of despair.

Am I enough? I question the air,
Every smile, every stare.
I've given all, but it slips away,
A shadow of hope that won't stay.
I fear to lose, though none has left,
The past keeps running every test.
I want to trust, but doubt persists,
Haunted by shadows that life insists.

I rehearse each word before it leaves,
Still fear twists the simplest deeds.

Every "I love you" feels like a test,
Every silence steals from my chest.
I think they'll leave, though they stay,
My past keeps shadows chasing me each day.
I measure trust with a careful scale,
Yet all my effort feels frail.
Each plan I make, each hope I hold,
Collapses quietly, never bold.
I fight my mind, I fight my heart,
But shadows of doubt play their part.
I want to lean, I want to fall,
But shadows of worth haunt it all.

What if my past doesn't define me?
What if trust could set me free?
The question lingers in the night,
Shadows flicker, half of the light.

Am I enough? The question remains,
Through every joy, through every pain.
I've given all, yet doubt still grips,
Life tests me with unyielding whips.
I want to trust, I want to stay,
But haunted by shadows, I fray.
Still I breathe, still I fight,
In the quiet shadow of the night.

Maybe one day I'll let it go,
Believe in the love I know.
Till then I stand, half afraid,
Haunted by shadows, in the choices I made.

Song Summary:

Living in constant anticipation of abandonment despite present stability, unable to trust that my marriage might follow a different pattern than previous relationships.

What I Was Actually Writing About:

Because I've had a lot of poor relationships in my life, romantic and platonic, I always ask if I'm enough? I feel like I'm not worth people's love and I feel like people are always going to leave me. I'm just a product of the moment, not a genuine connection. I live in constant anticipation of abandonment. Despite being married to someone who hasn't left, who shows up, who says they love me, I still can't trust that this might follow a different pattern than previous relationships. Every interaction gets filtered through the question in the title: Am I enough? Even when I get reassurance, I question whether it's genuine or provisional. Whether they mean it now but won't mean it later.

The Pattern/Mechanism:

The core tension is between present reality and internalized fear. Intellectually, I recognize that my wife hasn't abandoned me. Emotionally? I remain convinced it's inevitable. Past experiences created a lens through which all current affection appears temporary. I rehearse each word before it leaves my mouth. I treat the relationship as something fragile that requires perfect performance to maintain. If I say the wrong thing, if I'm not enough, if I fail to meet some invisible standard — that's when she'll leave. So I measure everything. Calculate every response. Try to be whatever version of myself will make her stay.

The Tension:

This hypervigilance transforms genuine moments into anxiety triggers. When my wife expresses care, I question whether it's genuine or obligatory. When there's silence, I interpret it as withdrawal — she's realizing she made a mistake, she's preparing to leave. Despite effort and self-awareness, I cannot escape these patterns. I know that I'm projecting past trauma onto present reality. I know she's not the people who left before. But knowing doesn't change that feeling. The fear lives in my body, not my mind, and it won't listen to reason.

Where I Am With This:

There's a faint hope that one day I'll let it go. That one day I'll trust that she's staying because she wants to, not despite me. But that hope remains distant, aspirational. For now, I exist in perpetual bracing. Half afraid. Unable to fully inhabit my marriage because I'm too busy preparing for it to end. Past relationships taught me that everyone leaves eventually. And I can't unlearn that lesson, even when the present contradicts it.

Nothing Feels

Every sound feels quiet inside my head.
Every thought's just noise I already said.
The light still shines, but I don't care.
The warmth is gone, but I'm still there.
No ache, no flame, no spark revealed—
Just breathing through what nothing feels.

I used to feel too much, now I feel none,
Numb from battles I thought I'd won.
Every word repeats like static replay,
Same regrets in a different day.
I plan my speech before I talk,
Map each path before I walk.
But still I end where silence waits,
Every move I make feels too late.
I don't cry, I just recall,
The details, the names, the downfall.
Every voice still echoes through,
But none of them sound like truth.
If sadness is heavy, then I'm its ghost,
Alive in body, but hollow the most.

I don't reach out, I just exist,
Drifting through what moments missed.
I thought I'd heal, but time congeals—
And nothing hurts, 'cause nothing feels.

Nothing feels, not pain, not peace,
The quiet hum will never cease.
I fade inside the calm I built,
A steady pulse beneath the guilt.
No fire left, no ice to thaw,
Just breathing out what once I saw.
It doesn't hurt, it doesn't heal,
It just exists—nothing feels.

I watch the days just fall in line,
Routine heartbeat marking time.

They ask me "how," I say "I'm fine,"
But "fine" means empty, not benign.
I used to drown in every thought,
Now I float through what I forgot.
Apathy's a calm disease,
It takes your breath, but lets you breathe.
I write down plans I never start,
Outline joy like it's an art.
They talk of love, I nod, I try,
But echoes fade before reply.
I'm not broken, I'm just sealed,
Protected by what can't be healed.

If feeling's gone, is that relief?
Or just a softer form of grief?
I keep on moving, slow but real—
Pretending that's what healing feels.

Nothing feels, and maybe that's fine,
At least the ache is not mine.
The world still turns, the sky still bleeds,
But I've outgrown what comfort needs.
No highs, no lows, no grand reveals,
Just quiet space where nothing feels.

Maybe numbness is my peace,
Maybe stillness is release.
If this is all that time conceals—
Then I'll learn to live
In what nothing feels.

Nothing Feels

Song Summary:
The transition from feeling too much to feeling nothing at all, where emotional absence becomes its own form of suffering.

What I Was Actually Writing About:
With all of my emotional trauma in my life, professionally, platonically, romantically, I've hit a point where nothing really feels to me anymore. My default emotion is apathy. I'm never happy, I'm not sad, I'm indifferent. When I was deployed to Afghanistan as a contractor I was near a large truck bomb that had detonated. I was numb to that experience and that numbness was terrifying. I no longer care what happens to me because of everything that's happened in my life. I transitioned from feeling too much to feeling none. What might look like peace or calm from the outside is actually emotional absence. A protective shutdown that has calcified into permanent disconnection—my apathy. The emptiness permeates everything. Sensory experiences still occur—the light still shines, things still happen around me—but they provoke no internal response. I operate on autopilot, going through the motions of life without any genuine engagement.

The Pattern/Mechanism:
This apathy evolved as a defense mechanism. I used to drown in every thought. Every emotion was overwhelming, consuming, too much to bear. So my system shut down. Numbness emerged as protection from pain. At first, the numbness was relief. No more drowning. No more overwhelming feelings. Just nothing. Quiet. Manageable. But that protection became its own prison. What started as a shield became walls I can't dismantle. Plans go unstarted because I can't access the motivation to begin them. Joy is something I can outline academically—I know theoretically what should make me happy—but I can't actually experience it. Love prompts only hollow acknowledgment. I know I'm supposed to feel something. I know objectively that I care. But the feeling isn't there.

The Tension:
Social interactions become performances. Someone asks "how are you?" I say "I'm fine." But "fine" doesn't mean wellness. It means emptiness. It means I've successfully made it through another day

without collapsing. The words come automatically, a script I've memorized so well I no longer need to think about the lines. I'm sealed off. That word captures both safety and suffocation. Protected from pain, yes. But also cut off from everything else. Connection. Joy. The full spectrum of human experience. Protected, but trapped. And I don't know if I can get back to feeling, even if I wanted to.

Where I Am With This:

Is this healing? Have I found some kind of equilibrium? Or is this just a softer form of grief—trading overwhelming pain for complete absence of feeling? The final commitment is to learn to live in what nothing feels. If emotional reconnection isn't possible—if I can't get back to feeling things the way I used to—then survival requires making peace with the void. Accepting that this might be as good as it gets. I don't know if that's acceptance or defeat. Maybe it's both.

I Remember

I remember words you don't recall,
Every promise, big or small.
I replay them quiet in my mind,
Trying to find what I left behind.
Every laugh feels like a scene,
I've memorized what it used to mean.
Some memories whisper, some just sigh,
They fade, but never say goodbye.

I remember everything I said too loud,
Every smile I gave to please the crowd.
I can quote the tone you used that night,
Down to pauses that didn't sound right.
I plan replies for things long gone,
Choreograph where I went wrong.
It's not regret — it's rehearsal,
Every silence feels reversal.
I try to move, but thought's too loud,
Peace is memory wrapped in shroud.
Every detail feels like proof,
That I could've changed the truth.

I can't forget, I can't forgive,
The way my mind won't let me live.
I try to rest, but my mind replays,
Every word I wish I'd phrased another way.

My mind don't fade — it archives pain,
Keeps every storm, forgets the rain.
I see the past in sharper hue,
Every color turned to residue.
I wish I could just let it go,
But I'm haunted by what I know.
Memory's kind but never kind enough,
It loves too deep, it hurts too much.

I build conversations in advance,
So I don't repeat a failed chance.

I play chess with words in sleep,
Guarding meaning I can't keep.
It's not obsession — it's survival,
Every memory's a quiet rival.
I don't move on — I move in loops,
Building echoes into proof.
What if forgetting is the cure?
What if memory just blurs?
I'd rather hurt than fade away,
So I let my echoes stay.

My mind replays till the silence breaks,
I live in the sound my memory makes.
Every second stretched too long,
Every right turned to wrong.
I can't escape the things I know,
They haunt me soft, they haunt me slow.
And when I fade beneath the glow,
I'll still be living in the echo.

Every sound fades, but mine repeats,
Every loss plays on repeat.
Memory's kind, but it won't let go—
I'm still living in the echo.

Song Summary:

The exhausting habit of obsessive memory that catalogues pain while forgetting peace, replaying conversations endlessly without resolution.

What I Was Actually Writing About:

I do not have a photographic memory. But when I was in the military I was tasked with remembering a vast amount of information. If you could recall information you could save lives. My childhood of identifying patterns and reacting to them helped me excel at this part of my job. Now I have this memory where I'm able to remember details that other people don't. So I see the looks people have, the tones they say things in. I read into these things and think that they're worse than they actually are. This leaves me questioning everything. One of my previous jobs required my memory to be impeccable. I don't have a photographic memory, but I remember things. Conversations with people. Small details that seemed irrelevant at the time. I can quote exchanges from years ago. Reconstruct scenes in precise detail. Replay interactions down to pauses that didn't sound right, shifts in tone, the exact words used. What might seem like a gift is actually a curse. While other people move on— forgetting the small moments and minor conflicts that comprise daily life—I remain trapped in endless review. Each remembered exchange becomes material for revision. A script to be rewritten mentally even though the moment has already passed and can't be changed.

The Pattern/Mechanism:

My mind operates as a relentless cataloging system that archives pain while forgetting peace. I remember every argument, every misunderstanding, every moment where I said the wrong thing or should have said something different. But the good moments? Those fade. Those blur. My brain doesn't catalogue joy the same way it catalogues mistakes. I rehearse conversations that will never happen. It's a compulsive replay, as if perfect analysis might retroactively alter what occurred. As if I could think hard enough about the past to change it. I recognize this pattern as a survival mechanism. In my previous job, the analysts who remembered, who noticed patterns, who could predict what was coming, were those

56

who saved lives. And the house I grew up in, when you remembered details, noticed patterns, you could predict what was coming—that helped us survive.

The Tension:
Memory provides illusory control while actually preventing presence and growth. I'm so busy reviewing what already happened that I can't fully engage with what's happening now. I understand I'm trapped in loops. I know this pattern keeps me stuck. But I view this as preferable to the alternative—losing those memories entirely. If I forget, if I let it fade, then it's like it never happened. And if it never happened, then I can't learn from it. Can't prepare for it happening again. Can't protect myself. So I stay haunted by what I know. I live in endless replay. It's exhausting. It prevents me from being present. But it's the only way my mind knows how to keep me safe.

Where I Am With This:
So I stay haunted by what I know. I live in endless replay. It's exhausting. It prevents me from being present. But it's the only way my mind knows how to keep me safe.

What Seems

A glance feels sharp, a word feels cold,
The story bends before it's told.
Lines twist and turn beneath my mind,
Truth hides somewhere I can't quite find.

A silent text can feel like a sting,
A passing look can warp everything.
Every small act lost in the middle,
Every quiet moment turns to a riddle.
Thoughts collide, my logic fights,
Shapes of meaning in shifting lights.
I spiral through what may or may not be,
A storm of signs only I can see.
The air feels heavy, the room feels tight,
A fleeting pause can cloud the sight.
Yet sometimes I glimpse a gentle hue,
The world is broader than my view.

Lines shift, the truth bend,
The story sways, the edges blend.
What seems harsh may be benign,
A flicker of clarity, slowly mine.

Things are never what they seem,
A fleeting shape, a tangled dream.
I chase the patterns in the air,
But meaning shifts, it's never bare.
Each misread sign, each tangled thought,
Reflects the battles my mind has fought.
The lens I hold can twist and bend,
But clarity can still ascend.

Every pause writes stories untold,
Every silence turns lukewarm to cold.
I weave the threads, I stitch the line,
But sometimes the pattern isn't mine.
The walls I build are only mine to see,

The sky outside is wider than me.
A stumble feels like a crack in stone,
Yet stones can shift and form a home.
Each fleeting doubt can teach me weight,
Each crooked turn can change my fate.
I bend and test, I push, I pause,
The world's reflection reveals its laws.

If I step back, the edges blur,
The storm dissolves, the mind concurs.
Not harsh, not cruel, just wider skies,
The world reshapes before my eyes.

Things are never what they seem,
The fleeting shape, the tangled dream.
Patterns fade, the mind unwinds,
A broader truth that softly shines.
Each misread sign, each tangled thought,
Teaches lessons I once forgot.
The lens I hold can twist and bend,
But understanding finds its end.

I step back, breathe, and see,
The world is wider than me.
Shapes shift, meanings blend,
A story's clarity finds its end.

Song Summary:
The automatic process of interpreting ordinary moments as evidence of impending loss or rejection, reading danger into everything.

What I Was Actually Writing About:
This is a follow up to I Remember in the sense that I see those tones and looks and I think the absolute worst thing possible. I have fear of abandonment and I have fear of rejection. So I have a tendency to doomsday prep for every situation and moments that are benign seem hostile. I exist in constant interpretation. A delayed text response, a passing glance, a moment of silence—all ordinary occurrences that get filtered through anxiety and reframed as evidence of impending loss or rejection. Nothing is just what it is. Everything means something. Every small action becomes a riddle requiring solving. Someone takes a few hours to text back? They're pulling away. Someone seems quiet? They're mad at me. Someone gives a short answer? They're done with this conversation. Here's the gap: I recognize that I'm constructing narratives before facts emerge. I know I'm doing this. But I cannot stop the automatic process.

The Pattern/Mechanism:
This is learned behavior. Past experiences trained me to anticipate danger, to search for warning signs, to never take safety at face value. The hypervigilance that once served as protection now manufactures threats from innocuous moments. The problem isn't that I'm bad at reading people. The problem is that I'm reading threat into everything, even when no threat exists. My mind defaults to searching for danger. I construct catastrophic narratives from minimal data. I turn neutral moments into evidence of abandonment or rejection. Here's the thing though—this cuts both ways. Just as benign moments can feel threatening, what seems harsh may actually be benign.

The Tension:
Sometimes a delayed text is just a delayed text. I know this intellectually. I understand that not everything carries hidden meaning. That people have their own lives, their own distractions, their own reasons for being quiet or brief that have nothing to do

with me. But knowing doesn't change the automatic response. My nervous system still reacts as if every small shift signals danger. My body remembers the house where silence meant something bad was coming. Where a certain tone meant get small, get quiet, get ready. That training doesn't disappear just because I'm not in that house anymore.

Where I Am With This:

Even with awareness, even with perspective, the automatic pattern of searching for danger remains difficult to overcome. My mind still defaults to threat. Still reads meaning into neutral moments. Still constructs catastrophic narratives from minimal data. I'm working on it. But decades of training don't disappear because I've identified the pattern.

Reason Enough

I'm not good enough, I can't, I don't, I fail,
Every step I take feels like I derail.
The life I made keeps testing me,
A mirror of what I struggle to be.

Every misstep I replay, every choice I regret,
I tell myself it's reason enough to forget.
I measure life in limits, counting every flaw,
The logic of my doubt is sharper than a saw.
I can't, I shouldn't, I never will,
My mind constructs the cage, it builds it still.
Even love I hold feels like it slips,
I justify the fear with tightened grips.
I plan my steps, but still I stumble,
Each inner voice makes my vision crumble.
The past becomes a rulebook, a harsh guide,
Every whisper of hope gets pushed aside.
I rationalize, I reason, I debate,
Build walls of "not enough" that suffocate.
And yet, a voice beneath the strain,
Questions the chains and calls my name.

Why not me? Why can't I?
I've given all, but still I try.
The doubts persist, but I resist,
A spark remains I can't dismiss.

I am worth it, I can break through,
The chains of doubt won't hold what's true.
I've justified the darkness for too long,
Now I reclaim my voice, I reclaim my song.
Each step I take, though gritty, earned,
A lesson learned, a corner turned.
I see the light, but still I fight,
Reason enough to hold on tight.

I question every "no," every closed door,
My mind spins logic, searching for more.

I've justified retreat, justified pain,
Justified silence to avoid the strain.
But what if I flipped the argument, turned it around,
The reasons I gave to quit can now be unbound?
I step forward, but still with care,
The past reminds me to beware.
Every stumble still leaves a mark,
But even scars can ignite a spark.
I'm learning to fight, to rise, to stand,
To take my worth into my own hands.
No perfect path, no flawless day,
But reason enough to find my way.

I am enough, I can't deny,
Even if the past tries to defy.
The road is long, the work remains,
But sparks of light outlast the chains.

I am worth it, I will break through,
The doubts can't define what I do.
I've justified the darkness, now I reclaim,
Each small victory lights the flame.
It's gritty, earned, each step I take,
A life rebuilt from the choices I make.
The fight continues, but now I see,
Reason enough resides in me.

The struggle lingers, but I still rise,
A spark persists beyond the lies.
I am worth it — and I know it's true,
Reason enough to start anew.

Song Summary:

The violent oscillations between feeling worthless and amazing, using reason as a weapon against myself.

What I Was Actually Writing About:

I have that bipolar view of feeling like I'm absolutely worthless to being incredibly awesome. I write these songs and I think to myself, "These are so good." Then I try to get other people to hear them, or I actually listen to the words myself and I'm like, "I'm not okay, this is not good." It's a violent oscillation between both extremes and to me I'm always floating between these two. I usually excel at the things I do, so when I'm met with resistance I'm always asking why am I not succeeding? This isn't about low self-esteem. It's about existing within a self-constructed cage of inadequacy, using logic and reason to justify my unworthiness. The constant negotiation between crushing doubt and emerging confidence. I meticulously catalog flaws. Replay missteps. Build elaborate justifications for why I don't deserve success or love. This intellectual framework of self-limitation feels rational. That's what makes it so effective. I'm not just feeling bad about myself—I'm constructing logical arguments for why I should feel bad about myself.

The Pattern/Mechanism:

The bipolar swing between worthlessness and worth continues. Some days I'm convinced I'm fundamentally inadequate. Some days I can see my value. But I've been using my capacity for reason against myself. The same analytical mind that builds cases for unworthiness can build cases for worth. The tool isn't the problem. The target is. If I can construct such convincing arguments for my inadequacy, I can redirect that same intellectual energy toward self-belief. Questions emerge that flip the script: "Why not me? Why can't I?" I begin to reclaim agency. Recognizing that the intellectual framework I've built doesn't have to serve self-destruction.

The Tension:

The resolution isn't stable triumph. It's ongoing struggle. The old patterns have decades of momentum. But now there's a competing voice. Now there's a counter-argument. Now the internal debate isn't just self-condemnation—it's negotiation. And negotiation means there's a chance. This is a daily choice to believe in myself despite the persistent pull of doubt. Not through feeling, but through reasoning. I'm learning to tip the scale toward self-acceptance by using the same logical framework that once destroyed me to now defend me. It's still a fight. But now the internal debate includes both prosecution and defense.

Where I Am With This:
I commit to fighting for self-worth rather than against it. That's the shift. Not from self-doubt to confidence. But from using my mind to destroy myself to using my mind to defend myself. It's still a fight. But now the internal debate includes both prosecution and defense.

Behind the Mask

I smile in the light, I nod with ease,
A quiet performance meant to appease.
The world sees calm, the world sees me strong,
But inside, the notes of pain play long.

Every word I speak is a careful line,
Each gesture polished, each glance refined.
I wear this mask to keep the peace,
Hiding the storm that never seems to cease.
The laughs I share, the smiles I feign,
Cover the aches, the hidden strain.
Even those I love don't always know,
The weight I carry, the undertow.
I glance around, see masks on all,
A gallery of shadows against the wall.
We nod, we talk, we seem just fine,
Each soul a secret, a hidden sign.

What if we dared to take it off,
The mask that shields, the polished cloth?
A fleeting truth, a quiet glance,
A shared connection, a second chance.

We all wear masks, we all pretend,
Hiding the sorrow we can't defend.
Behind the smile, behind the gaze,
Are hearts that ache in private ways.
If we show the cracks, the fear, the strain,
We find the ones who feel the same.
A quiet truth, a hand to hold,
The masks come off, the stories told.

I walk through crowds, a face composed,
A practiced calm, carefully posed.
Inside, the chaos churns and fights,
A quiet battle through endless nights.
Yet sometimes I catch a fleeting sign,
Someone else's shadow mirrors mine.

The mask feels heavy, the mask feels real,
But small glimpses show what others feel.
We hide, we shift, we guard, we bend,
But empathy waits around the bend.
The more we share, the more we find,
The common threads that bind mankind.

A mask removed reveals the heart,
A fragile piece, a work of art.
Together we show what's often concealed,
And in that truth, a bond is healed.

We all wear masks, we all pretend,
Hiding the sorrow we can't defend.
Behind the smile, behind the gaze,
Are hearts that ache in private ways.
If we dare to share, to let it show,
We find the hearts that also glow.
A quiet truth, a hand to hold,
The masks come off, the stories told.

I take a breath, I drop the guise,
See the world through honest eyes.
The masks we wear, the pain we hide,
Can fade when we walk side by side.

Song Summary:

The recognition that everyone is performing composure while hiding their pain, creating isolation through collective pretense.

What I Was Actually Writing About:

I know I'm not the only one who has feelings like what I've explained so far. I know other people have issues and demons in their past. This is my attempt at acknowledging these things in other people. We're all wearing this mask of being okay when we're really not. We're all hiding something that's bothering us because I feel that society tells us to keep that to ourselves. I acknowledge my own performative existence. The carefully constructed facade of calm and capability that conceals inner turmoil. But this isn't confession of personal deception so much as observation of collective survival strategy. I'm not uniquely fake. We're all performing. I look around and I don't see genuine contentment. I recognize that others are equally engaged in hiding their pain. Every polished interaction, every casual "I'm fine," every composed exterior potentially conceals the same weight, the same undertow of struggle. This reframes everything. What felt like personal inadequacy—I'm the only one struggling, I'm uniquely broken—transforms into common experience. It's not that I'm failing at life while everyone else succeeds. It's that we're all struggling, and we're all hiding it.

The Pattern/Mechanism:

Social media has made this exponentially worse. We're all curating highlight reels. Posting the victories, the aesthetics, the moments that suggest we have it all together. Everyone's feed looks like they've figured life out. But that's just another mask—a digital one. We're all performing for an audience now, not just in person but constantly, publicly, creating this feedback loop where everyone thinks everyone else is fine, which makes us hide our struggles even more. The masks create isolation. The performance prevents genuine connection. Nobody can support you if they don't know you need support. Nobody can say "me too" if you never show them what you're carrying.

The Tension:

Yet the masks also serve protective functions. We navigate social spaces that don't make room for authentic struggle. The mask isn't just dishonesty—it's adaptation to environments that punish authenticity. But what if we risked showing the weight? If everyone is secretly struggling, then showing cracks doesn't expose unique weakness. It invites authentic connection. The solution isn't fixing internal problems. The solution is dismantling the collective pretense that prevents people from recognizing their shared experience. When one person drops the mask, it gives permission for others to drop theirs. And suddenly you're not alone in the struggle. You're connected through it.

Where I Am With This:

The solution isn't fixing internal problems. The solution is dismantling the collective pretense that prevents people from recognizing their shared experience. When one person drops the mask, it gives permission for others to drop theirs. And suddenly you're not alone in the struggle. You're connected through it. Maybe the problem isn't that we're broken. Maybe the problem is that we've all agreed to pretend we're not. Maybe connection requires breaking that agreement.

Connected

I look around, it feels like I'm alone,
Each heart a world I've never known.
But in the silence, I hear a thread,
Whispers of the words that go unsaid.

I've felt the ache of standing still,
The quiet fear I can't fulfill.
Thought no one sees the cracks I hide,
The doubts that rattle deep inside.
But maybe others feel the same,
A lonely fire behind their name.
The faces pass, the eyes don't lie,
We're all just learning how to try.
Every pause, every whispered thought,
A bridge to show we're not forgot.
The world feels heavy, but we're aligned,
A thread of hope through heart and mind.

If we reach out, speak what's true,
We'll see ourselves in others too.
The lonely hearts, the anxious mind,
A common thread we all can find.

We're all a little lonely, a little unsure,
But together in ways we can't ignore.
The fears we carry, the tears we hide,
Are mirrored everywhere, far and wide.
Even when apart, we share the road,
The silent burdens, the quiet load.
Reach out your hand, let someone in,
We're not alone — together we begin.

I've counted nights where hope felt thin,
Felt like a stranger inside my skin.
But looking close, I see the spark,
In every eye, a beating heart.
The quiet smiles, the gentle nods,
The shared mistakes, the unseen odds.

All our flaws, our silent pleas,
Are carried softly on the breeze.
We stumble, fall, and rise again,
The lonely path that we all wend.
But when we speak, when we connect,
We find our strength, our shared respect.

No one stands alone in truth,
Each soul reflects another's youth.
Our fears, our joys, our quiet pain,
All woven together like gentle rain.

We're all a little lonely, a little unsure,
But together in ways we can't ignore.
The fears we carry, the tears we hide,
Are mirrored everywhere, far and wide.
Even when apart, we share the road,
The silent burdens, the quiet load.
Reach out your hand, let someone in,
We're not alone — together we begin.

I see the world and know it's true,
The lonely heart is me and you.
Every fear, every quiet plea,
Together, we are finally free.

Song Summary:
The invitation to drop the mask and reach out from the broken place, recognizing that shared struggle creates the foundation for authentic connection.

What I Was Actually Writing About:
This song is about dropping my mask and showing people I'm not okay. That I feel all of these things. These were the first songs I wrote and to me these allow me to express myself in ways that I was never able to express before. Sharing these songs with people is my showing everyone else that these feelings are real, you may have them as well, so let's celebrate what makes us broken because hiding it doesn't do anything but make us feel more alone. Where previous songs explored these struggles as solitary burdens, "Connected" moves from introspective examination to active seeking. The central premise is that vulnerability creates the pathway to belonging. I recognize that my specific struggles—the anxiety, the numbness, the fear of abandonment, the oscillating self-worth—these aren't aberrations. They're variations on universal human themes. The loneliness. The doubt. The persistent feeling of being "a little unsure." These aren't evidence of fundamental brokenness. They're shared conditions of being human. Maybe everyone feels this way, at least sometimes. Maybe I'm not uniquely damaged. Maybe this is just what it means to be alive and aware and carrying weight.

The Pattern/Mechanism:
Rather than presenting these as problems requiring solutions before connection can occur, I suggest these are precisely the commonalities that make connection possible. Authenticity about struggle becomes the language of genuine relationship. Not pretending we're fine. Not waiting until we're fixed. But reaching out from the broken place and finding others in broken places too. This is me dropping my mask completely. Presenting my documented pain as testament and test. By opening up fully through this collection, I'm seeking recognition. Hoping others will respond with "me too" rather than judgment.

The Tension:

This is why I wrote this collection. Not to document my healing. Not to inspire others with my triumph. But to reach out from my broken place and say: if you feel this too, you're not alone. You don't have to be fixed to be worthy of connection. You don't have to have it figured out to deserve belonging. You just have to be willing to drop the mask. To reach out. To say "this is what I'm carrying" and trust that someone else will say "me too." Maybe the problem isn't that we're broken. Maybe the problem is that we've all agreed to pretend we're not. Maybe connection requires breaking that agreement.

Where I Am With This:

The collection ends here. Not with resolution. Not with healing. Not with triumph over the struggles. But with invitation. With connection. With the recognition that maybe we're all broken, and maybe that's okay, and maybe we can find something resembling freedom in being broken together.

Collection II

Weight of Me

This is the collection about being called strong when you're disintegrating. About accomplishing things nobody notices or cares about. About carrying weight that's invisible to everyone else and realizing you've stopped expecting anyone to see it. This is about the exhausting work of survival—not living, just surviving—and discovering that's the only thing you know how to do. This is about the cost of endurance nobody talks about.

What This Collection Is

This collection is about what happens when you stop reaching for connection and start claiming solitary strength instead. It's the shift from "please see me" to "I don't need you to see me—I'll carry this myself."

Where the first collection reached tentatively toward others, hoping connection might heal, this one turns inward. Not because connection failed, but because I realized nobody else can carry this weight for me. I have to become strong enough to bear it alone. And I did. But strength through suffering is a cold kind of victory.

This collection charts a journey from hidden suffering through existential drift toward hard-won resilience. It opens with concealed pain, moves through various manifestations of disconnection and compensatory behaviors, confronts inherited trauma and perpetual searching, then concludes with defiant recognition of survival and readiness.

Unlike Collection I's movement toward vulnerable connection with others, Collection II moves toward self-recognition and solitary strength—finding power not in shared struggle but in acknowledged endurance.

Key Themes

The Performance of Normalcy: I've mastered the art of seeming fine—life looks stable from outside—but this successful performance creates radical isolation. Nobody sees the storm because the mask is too convincing, yet removing the mask feels impossible because the hidden struggle has become integrated into my identity.

Solitary Burden as Identity: Unlike Collection I where isolation was painful consequence, here I've made my hidden suffering into a defining characteristic. The weight isn't just carried—it's claimed as "part of me," a source of secret strength and distinction. There's complex pride woven through the pain: I survive what others couldn't, endure privately, prove resilience through silent persistence.

The Impossibility of Recognition: A profound loneliness emerges from the gap between internal experience and external perception. When I share achievements, others respond with indifference. When I look for validation, it doesn't materialize. This creates a feedback loop: sharing doesn't produce connection, so concealment continues, but concealment ensures continued invisibility.

Inherited Trauma: I look in the mirror and see the person who hurt me. Their anger in my anger. Their control in my control. Can I escape what's written in my genes, my formative environment? The collection suggests painful truth: I'm inevitably shaped by my origins even when I reject them, and wholeness requires integrating rather than denying this inheritance.

Chronic Displacement: I experience persistent sense of being in the wrong place—capable of more, suited for elsewhere, perpetually misaligned with circumstances. Jobs don't fit, purposes remain elusive, belonging never materializes. This creates exhausting restlessness where every position feels temporary, every path provisional. The searching itself becomes the only constant.

Compensatory Behaviors: Faced with numbness and disconnection, I develop elaborate strategies to feel something—chasing dopamine through consumption, projecting hope into future plans, constantly creating targets to pursue. These aren't solutions but management techniques, ways to stay marginally engaged with existence when genuine emotion has shut down.

The Spiral of Overthinking: Mental hyperactivity emerges as both coping mechanism and additional burden. My mind becomes simultaneously protector (analyzing threats, preparing responses) and tormentor (generating endless catastrophic scenarios, preventing rest). Overthinking doesn't produce clarity; it creates paralysis while maintaining the illusion of control.

Survival as Achievement: The collection's resolution reframes endurance itself as victory. Not thriving, not happiness, not connection—simply continuing to exist despite accumulated damage becomes the measure of success. I claim my suffering as training, my scars as credentials, my continued standing as evidence of strength.

Why I Wrote This

I wrote this collection when I realized nobody was coming to save me. Connection hadn't healed me. Time hadn't healed me. Understanding hadn't healed me. So I had to become strong enough to carry the weight myself, indefinitely, without expecting it to ever get lighter.

There's something both empowering and devastating about that realization. Empowering because I discovered I'm capable of more than I thought—I can survive things that should have broken me. Devastating because I realized I'm going to have to keep surviving them, possibly forever, possibly alone.

I was angry when I wrote these. Angry at my father for what he did. Angry at my mother for what she didn't do. Angry at the toxic relationships that exploited wounds I didn't know I had. Angry at myself for carrying patterns I swore I'd never repeat. Angry that I couldn't just be normal, couldn't just be happy, couldn't just fucking rest.

But underneath the anger was something colder: acceptance. Not peace—acceptance. This is who I am now. This is what trauma made me. I'm not going to transcend it. I'm going to weaponize it. Turn the damage into armor. Make the survival itself the victory.

The Emotional Journey

This collection operates in registers of weariness, defiance, and grim determination. There's profound exhaustion—from maintaining appearances, from searching without finding, from surviving repeated blows—yet this fatigue coexists with stubborn refusal to surrender.

Isolation pervades but takes different form than Collection I's lonely yearning for connection. Here isolation becomes almost chosen, a consequence of carrying weight others can't comprehend and therefore can't share. There's pride mixed with the suffering—I take harsh satisfaction in my capacity to endure what breaks others, even as I acknowledge the cost.

Rage appears specifically in relation to my father, a hot emotion in an otherwise controlled landscape. The fury at seeing despised traits in myself provides intense feeling that contrasts with the numbness described elsewhere.

The final pieces introduce something like warrior acceptance—not happiness but claiming of battle-earned strength. There's fierce ownership of survival, transformation of victim narrative into survivor identity.

The Arc

Where it starts: Hidden suffering. I carry weight nobody sees while appearing perfectly functional.

Where it moves: Achievement without recognition. Looking in the mirror and seeing the abuser. Searching for purpose that never materializes. Chasing sensations to feel alive. Spiraling in endless mental loops.

Where it bottoms out: The exhaustion of constantly questioning every choice, every path, the fundamental question of whether any of this matters.

Where it arrives: Still standing. Beaten, scarred, exhausted—but standing. Claiming that survival, that endurance, as its own form of strength. Not because it's beautiful but because it's real.

This collection argues that some people don't get the luxury of healing, of lightness, of easy joy. Instead, they get strength. They get the knowledge that they've already survived the worst. They get to stand, scarred and exhausted, and recognize that their continued standing—however ungraceful, however costly—is itself a form of triumph.

This is survival not as prelude to thriving but as its own valid endpoint. I've stopped waiting to feel better and started claiming what I've become through endurance. It's a harder, colder resolution than Collection I's reach toward connection, but it's equally valid— a different path through trauma that leads not to community but to fortress self, not to healing but to hardening, not to peace but to preparedness.

Content Warning

This collection deals with emotional numbness, depression, anxiety, compensation through substance/behavior, inherited trauma, seeing the abuser in yourself, existential displacement, suicidal ideation, and the weaponization of wounds. The tone is significantly colder and harder than the first collection—less yearning, more resignation. Less hope for connection, more grim determination to survive alone.

There's rage here too—at the parent who damaged me, at myself for carrying their traits, at a world that doesn't recognize what I've endured.

They Don't Know

I walk these rooms with a quiet face,
Hiding storms that no one can trace.
The weight I carry, they'll never see,
It fuels me, it's part of me.

They think I'm calm, they think I'm fine,
But I hold a storm beneath the line.
Every laugh I give, every smile I show,
Masks a fire that they'll never know.
I've felt the nights that twist the mind,
A shadow I keep so I won't unwind.
Shame locks the door, but it keeps me in place,
A part of who I am, I can't erase.
Some say "move on," some say "let it go,"
But the depth of my struggle they'll never know.
It drives my hands, it drives my pace,
This hidden weight shapes every space.

They don't know what I've walked through,
The nights that taught me to see it through.
Even if unseen, it's my guiding thread,
A force that lives in the life I've led.

I hold the weight they'll never see,
Every step I take proves what I can be.
I stand in silence, I rise in the dark,
This is my strength, my hidden spark.

I've carried burdens that shaped my way,
Guided my steps through night and day.
I learned to smile while the ground shifted,
Every gesture a layer, carefully lifted.
I keep it secret, a power and shame,
A quiet companion, yet fuels my aim.
Without this weight, I wouldn't know,
The person I am, the strength I show.
Every whispered thought I hold inside,
Is a thread in the life I quietly guide.

They see the surface, the calm, the glow,
But the depth beneath, they'll never know.

It's quiet, it's heavy, it's mine alone,
A hidden force that I've always known.
I don't share it, yet it makes me whole,
This unseen weight defines my soul.

I hold the weight they'll never see,
Every step I take proves what I can be.
I stand in silence, I rise in the dark,
This is my strength, my hidden spark.

I'll walk this path, though they don't see,
It's mine alone, my quiet victory.
Alone in this, yet I won't bend,
The journey remains, my steps don't end.

Song Summary:
Moving through life wearing a mask of composure while carrying storms that remain completely hidden from everyone around me.

What I Was Actually Writing About:
This song is a result of a conversation I had with my sister in law several years ago. She said something about how I don't know her trauma, and that I couldn't relate to her. She was right that I didn't know her trauma, but she didn't know the demons in my past, my trauma, my pain. If she knew what I held inside she may have been more understanding. I move through life wearing a mask of composure while carrying storms that remain completely hidden. My life appears functional from the outside. Achievements visible, composure maintained, social interactions managed. But this surface-level competence obscures profound internal turmoil. Every laugh and smile serves as camouflage. This creates a peculiar loneliness: surrounded by people who believe everything is fine while I'm drowning in pain that goes unwitnessed. The casual advice of others reveals how completely they misunderstand the magnitude of what I'm carrying. I exist in a private reality of nights that twist the mind, experiences that have fundamentally shaped who I am but remain completely invisible to those around me.

The Pattern/Mechanism:
The hidden struggle has become both burden and identity. The weight isn't just carried—it's integrated. It's part of me. It shapes decisions, drives pace, fuels ambition. There's a complex relationship with this concealed pain: it's both shame that locks the door and a guiding thread. I derive some sense of purpose or strength from my ability to endure silently. The secrecy becomes its own form of power—a hidden spark—proof of resilience that only I can recognize. This is a victory celebrated alone, witnessed by no one, a strength that must remain secret to be maintained.

The Tension:
Yet there's profound weariness beneath the stoicism. I stand in silence. I rise in the dark. But the emphasis on solitude underscores the cost: maintaining this mask means no one can truly know me. The strength I've built through silent endurance also ensures I

remain isolated in my pain. The very mechanism that helps me survive—the ability to hide what I'm carrying—prevents the connection that might ease the burden. People see composure and assume I'm fine. They give casual advice about moving on, letting go, not knowing the depth of what I hold. And I can't tell them. Because telling them means showing weakness. And showing weakness feels like death.

Where I Am With This:

I continue to carry the weight in silence. The mask remains in place. The storm stays hidden. This is how I've learned to survive.

Alone in This

I've climbed a mountain no one else can see,
Carved a river flowing only for me.
The weight feels heavy when it goes unseen,
I'm proud, but alone, caught in between.

I laid the stones in silence, step by step,
Built a path I hoped someone would accept.
Each victory quiet, a whisper in the hall,
Hoping someone notices before it all falls.

Hands reach out, but they brush right past,
My joy feels small when their glance doesn't last.
I wanted them to see the work I've done,
Instead I'm left counting shadows in the sun.
Every success, a trophy in the dark,
I shout inside, but it leaves no mark.
I second-guess the pride I dare to hold,
Is it a gift or just a story untold?
I reach, but the echoes fall back cold,
Energy mismatched, my steps feel old.
Is it me, or do they just not see?
All I wanted was to share this with me.

Alone in this, my mountain stands tall,
I hoped for company, but I climb it all.
I show, I give, I hope someone cares,
But pride is heavy when no one shares.

I built a river through my own lands,
Every current shaped by my hands.
The banks are strong, the flow is mine,
But no one wades in the water I design.
I trace the course, the journey alone,
The bridges I raised, the seeds I've sown.
Do I celebrate for me, or for the crowd?
The silence answers, it's neither loud.
I weigh my steps, uncertain, unsure,
Every accomplishment feels obscure.

Yet even in quiet, I know what I've done,
Even alone, the path can't be undone.

Maybe pride is a note that fades unheard,
Maybe applause is quiet, just inside my words.
Even if unseen, I hold it true,
A path I paved, my own breakthrough.

Alone in this, my mountain stands tall,
I hoped for company, but I climb it all.
I show, I give, I hope someone cares,
But pride is heavy when no one shares.

I'll walk this path, though they don't see,
It's mine alone, my quiet victory.
Alone in this, yet I won't bend,
The journey remains, my steps don't end.

Song Summary:
The painful experience of achievement without recognition, climbing mountains no one else can see.

What I Was Actually Writing About:
This one is about how I feel like I accomplish things that go unnoticed. There's days when I feel like I cannot get out of bed. I just want to stay in bed, pull the blanket over my head and hide from the world. Some days just the act of getting out of bed is something I achieve. Other days I do some chores around the house, or I work out, or I accomplish something at work that had been bugging me for days. These little victories are things that I'm proud of and when I get excited about them, I show some emotion after not showing any at all, my emotions are not met with any sort of reciprocal emotions. So my victories are met with silence. I accomplish something significant — climb a mountain no one else can see — but when shared, it's met with indifference or perfunctory acknowledgment rather than genuine enthusiasm. The central anguish is the mismatch between internal significance and external response. I've invested tremendous effort — laid the stones in silence, step by step — building something meaningful, hoping others would recognize its value. Yet hands reach out but brush right past. My joy feels small when their glance doesn't last. The accomplishment itself remains real, but without witness or validation, it feels incomplete.

The Pattern/Mechanism:
There's painful vulnerability in the repeated attempts to share. I show, I give, I hope someone cares. Each lukewarm response compounds the isolation. The lack of external validation doesn't just disappoint — it causes me to question whether my own assessment of worth is accurate. The spiraling self-doubt: Are people truly disinterested, or unable to understand what was achieved? Is the accomplishment actually less impressive than I believed, or is there an energy mismatch where others can't perceive what I see? I second-guess the pride I dare to hold. Is it a gift or just a story untold?

The Tension:

The closing verses attempt to reclaim agency and self-validation. Maybe pride is a note that fades unheard. Maybe applause is quiet, just inside my words. I wrestle with whether external validation is necessary for achievement to matter, tentatively concluding that even if unseen, I hold it true. But the persistent refrain—alone in this—underscores that this self-validation, however philosophically sound, doesn't fully compensate for the human need to have accomplishments witnessed and celebrated by others. The journey remains meaningful, but the solitude of that meaning weighs heavily. I continue creating, continue achieving, continue hoping someone will see what I've built. But mostly, I do it alone.

Where I Am With This:

The journey remains meaningful, but the solitude of that meaning weighs heavily. I continue creating, continue achieving, continue hoping someone will see what I've built. But mostly, I do it alone.

The Mirror Between Us

I see a stranger in the glass,
Eyes that look but never ask.
There's a silence I can't outlast,
And it sounds a lot like me.

I keep my voice low when I talk to myself,
Like I'm scared what the echo might tell.
Been patchin' my wounds with reason and rhyme,
But the cut still bleeds through time.
Every line in my face feels borrowed,
Every spark of rage, a debt I swallowed.
Try to build calm with my hands so steady,
But my fists remember before I'm ready.
I see thunder hidin' under my skin,
A ghost that grins when I give in.
Try to drown him out in a flood of grace,
But he knows my name — same blood, same face.

There's a tremor in my breath,
Like the storm forgot to die.
Every time I think I'm healing,
I see him in my eyes.

The mirror between us, breaking slow,
Pieces fall where I won't go.
I'm fighting a shadow I can't undo,
And every crack still shows the truth.

I bite my tongue just to feel control,
But that fire's a language I already know.
Been preachin' peace, but I keep score,
Prayin' my silence evens the war.
I trace my pulse — it beats too loud,
It echoes a man I disavowed.
Still, a part of him holds onto my spine,
The strength, the spite — both mine.
You can't unlearn the way you were built,
You just learn to stand without the guilt.

And maybe that's what mercy means —
To forgive the ghost inside your genes.

If I could start again, would I even change?
Or would I still be born from pain?
Some nights I think he's fading slow,
But it's me that won't let go.

The mirror between us starts to clear,
And I face the weight I used to fear.
I'm not him, but I'm not free,
He's the part that still made me.

The glass stops shaking, I finally see,
Not all that's broken remains in me.
The man I hate, the man I've grown —
Both reflections I call my own.

Song Summary:
Seeing the reflection of a despised parent in yourself, encountering the ghost of a man you hate yet cannot escape.

What I Was Actually Writing About:
I have photographs of myself around my house of me and my kids, enjoying the moment we were in. When I see these pictures all I can see are certain physical traits of my father. My father was an abusive man who would not only physically hurt us, but also emotionally. So I see him in me and I become hyper aware of things that I do that he did. When I lose my temper, when my first reaction is to shout instead of listen, when that rage inside me builds, I think of him and I can't shake it. I hate my father and we have things in common and I hate those parts of me. I look in the mirror and encounter not just my own face but the ghost of my father, a man I hate and loathe, yet cannot escape because his presence lives within my own body, mannerisms, and reflexes. The central torment is the involuntary inheritance of traits I've fought to reject. Every line in my face feels borrowed. Every spark of rage, a debt I swallowed. Physical features and emotional responses carry his signature, making my own body feel like foreign territory. There's thunder hiding under my skin— volatile impulses that mirror his behavior. Despite conscious efforts toward calm and control, my fists remember before I'm ready. The patterns are deeply ingrained.

The Pattern/Mechanism:
There's self-loathing in seeing his traits emerge, but also an inability to completely dissociate. I'm fighting a shadow I can't undo, and every crack still shows the truth. I want to believe I've transcended my origin—I disavowed him—yet I acknowledge that a part of him holds onto my spine. This isn't just about resemblance but about the internalization of both the strength and the spite. Even despised sources shape who we become. Questions of agency and destiny emerge: If I could start again, would I even change? Or would I still be born from pain? There's resignation in recognizing that you cannot unlearn the way you were built, that formative experiences leave permanent marks.

The Tension:

I can be both "not him" and simultaneously shaped by him. His influence is undeniable, present in my body and my reflexes and my rage. Yet I fight against becoming him. I resist the patterns even as I recognize their presence. The battle isn't to erase his influence — that's impossible — but to choose different responses despite the ingrained impulses. When I feel that thunder building under my skin, when my fists remember before I'm ready, I have to make a choice. I can let the pattern play out — become him in that moment — or I can break it. Most days I break it. But the effort of breaking it, over and over, is exhausting. And I hate that I have to fight at all.

Where I Am With This:

The closing verses attempt a painful reconciliation: Maybe that's what mercy means — to forgive the ghost inside your genes. The final image of the mirror beginning to clear suggests tentative peace — not erasing his presence but integrating it. Not all that's broken remains in me offers hope that inherited patterns don't have to define the future, even as both reflections I call my own acknowledges the permanent duality. This is acceptance without absolution.

Searching For Purpose

I thought I knew the road I'd take,
Every plan a promise I couldn't break.
Now the maps are gone, the signs unclear,
I ask myself, what am I here for, here?

I chased the visions that I thought were mine,
Built my dreams on the edge of time.
Every step forward, every path I paved,
Felt solid at first, then turned to waves.
I thought I had the answers, I thought I knew,
But the ground shifted, and so did the view.
Plans unravel, certainty fades,
I'm left in the echoes of my own cascade.
Who am I now? What do I hold?
Is purpose a story, or truth untold?
I reach for meaning on fragile land,
Grasping for footprints I can't understand.

The stars I followed vanish in the night,
Every guide I trusted fades from sight.
I search for a signal, a sign, a place,
A path to steady me, a quiet grace.

I'm searching for purpose, lost in the rain,
Every plan scattered, every gain in vain.
I question my path, I question my name,
Trying to find myself amidst the strain.

I thought my hands could shape the sky,
Now they're empty, wondering why.
Every blueprint, every goal I drew,
Seems like echoes when I review.
I feel the pull of unknown tides,
A current stronger than my pride.
I stumble, I falter, I ask again,
Will I ever know where this road will end?
I've walked through trials, I've felt the cost,
I've gained some, but I've also lost.

The questions linger, they never cease,
Is this search for purpose, or just for peace?

Perhaps the meaning isn't in the prize,
But in the journey, the lows, the highs.
Even when lost, the path remains,
Every step forward, every strain.

I'm searching for purpose, lost in the rain,
Every plan scattered, every gain in vain.
I question my path, I question my name,
Trying to. find myself amidst the strain.

I don't have the answers, I don't see the end,
But I keep moving, I keep around the bend.
Perhaps the journey is all I own,
A path unknown, but mine alone.

Song Summary:

The disorienting experience of chronic professional displacement and unfulfilled potential, constantly shifting between roles that never quite fit.

What I Was Actually Writing About:

I've moved through my life excelling at a lot of different things. Things I don't care about, things I'm not passionate about, and things I actually have an interest in. But I have never been able to find something where I felt like I belonged. When I was in the military I felt like I had a purpose. I was working as part of a team, my opinion was valued, I was celebrated for my work, and when I got out of the military I lost all of that. I've spent a long time searching for something to fill the void of what the military was to me. The military gave me the ability to escape my childhood and gave me a new perspective that allowed me to really see how things were when I was a child. It opened my eyes to what I had been through. So since getting out of the military I have bounced from job to job, always looking to recapture that magic. I had found something that really made me feel special but then I lost that due to circumstances outside of my control. When I lost that job I really took an emotional hit and I still haven't fully recovered. I move through life without a stable sense of vocational identity, constantly shifting between roles that never quite fit, always sensing I'm capable of more but unable to locate where that "more" might exist. The central frustration is the gap between perceived capability and actual placement. I feel I possess skills, vision, and capacity beyond what my current circumstances demand or recognize, yet I cannot find the environment where those qualities would be valued.

The Pattern/Mechanism:

The exhausting cycle of hope and disappointment. Every plan scattered, every gain in vain. I invest effort in building toward something, only to have it unravel. Each new job or opportunity initially promises to be the answer, felt solid at first, then turned to waves, only to reveal itself as another ill-fitting temporary stop. This pattern breeds deep existential questioning: Who am I now? What do I hold? Is purpose a story, or truth untold? The repeated relocations and professional shifts erode confidence in any stable identity, leaving me grasping for footprints I can't understand.

The Tension:

There's profound vulnerability in admitting this ongoing disorientation. The stars I followed vanish in the night. Every guide I trusted fades from sight. The markers that once provided direction have proven unreliable, leaving me without clear signals about where I belong or what I should be pursuing. The searching itself becomes exhausting: lost in the rain, questioning not just career path but fundamental identity—I question my name. Still, the underlying ache remains: the sense of capability without application, of belonging nowhere while suspecting there must be somewhere that fits. The military gave me that sense of belonging once. And I've been chasing that feeling ever since, never quite finding it again.

Where I Am With This:

The closing verses attempt to reframe the search itself as potentially meaningful. Perhaps the meaning isn't in the prize, but in the journey, the lows, the highs. There's tentative acceptance that purpose might not be a destination to arrive at but rather something that emerges through continued movement: Perhaps the journey is all I own, a path unknown, but mine alone.

Almost Alive

I tried the sweetness, it fades too soon,
Another fix beneath the moon.
Chasing warmth through paper skies,
But nothing burns, it just survives.

Feel the void where the spark should live,
Touch the flame, but it won't give.
Tried sugar, smoke, and a bitter pill,
Still can't find what makes me still.
Every high's just a higher fall,
Echoed laughs in an empty hall.
Pressure builds where feeling's gone,
Heartbeat flat but the mask stays on.
Caught in the chase of a phantom taste,
Another round, another waste.
If pain's the price, then charge it twice,
I'll pay in scars just to feel alive.

Is there something left in me to break?
Some small wound I've yet to fake?
I'm begging for the burn to start,
Just to prove I still have a heart.

I'm almost alive — for a fleeting night,
A flicker in the darkness, a shadow of the light.
It's not peace, it's just relief,
But I'll take the taste, however brief.

Tried numb, tried gone, tried "better than this,"
But silence don't answer, it just exists.
Can't fake joy, can't fake pain,
So I dance with ghosts to feel again.
Every smile's a stitched-up lie,
Every tear's just dust too dry.
If I can't feel love, I'll settle for fear,
At least it proves that I'm still here.
Bruised by comfort, torn by need,
Every craving a twisted creed.

I don't want joy — I want the ache,
That perfect cut no calm can fake.

I touch the flame and it feels like truth,
Even pain can feel like proof.
If it hurts, then maybe I'm real,
If it bleeds, then maybe I heal.

I'm almost alive — and that's enough to stay,
A borrowed thrill to light my way.
Don't need forever, don't need peace,
Just one more hit of sweet release.

And when the silence pulls me back,
I'll crave the pain I thought I lacked.
Almost alive, just for tonight,
One last breath before the light.

Song Summary:

The desperate pursuit of sensation in the face of emotional numbness, chasing fleeting highs to combat the persistent void.

What I Was Actually Writing About:

Because of my emotional state I find myself always looking for something that will give me that quick release of dopamine to feel something, anything. Whether it's pain or pleasure. I'll reach for junk food or soft drinks, I'll lock myself in my room with adult content, I'll do yard work knowing my back will hurt afterwards. I just want to feel something so I know I'm alive. When I was younger I used to do more self-harm. I'm no longer in that state of mind, but there were times when I was in such a bad emotional space that I would make myself bleed just so I could feel. I shocked some of my military supervisors when they saw my arms. I knew how to wear that mask that says I'm okay. I chase fleeting highs to combat the persistent void. Unable to access genuine joy or sustained emotion, I turn to immediate gratification—sugar, impulse purchases, any stimulus that can penetrate the apathy and provide momentary proof of being alive. These aren't pleasures. They're survival tactics, brief interruptions in an otherwise flat emotional landscape. The central dynamic is the addiction to temporary relief. I cycle through various sources of stimulation—not seeking happiness but simply trying to feel still, to achieve any internal response that confirms my existence.

The Pattern/Mechanism:

Every high's just a higher fall. Diminishing returns: each hit provides briefer relief, requires more to achieve the same effect, leaves me lower than before. There's haunting awareness of the futility. Nothing burns, it just survives. The fixes don't actually ignite anything lasting, they merely help me endure. The song perfectly captures this half-existence: not truly living but also not quite dead, sustained by borrowed thrills that provide just enough sensation to continue. It's not peace, it's just relief. But I'll take the taste, however brief.

The Tension:

A disturbing willingness to embrace pain as preferable to numbness. If I can't feel love, I'll settle for fear. At least it proves that I'm still here. This represents a profound departure from typical human motivation—not pursuing pleasure but pursuing anything that registers internally. I don't want joy—I want the ache. That perfect cut no calm can fake. I've become so desperate for sensation that suffering becomes desirable. Even pain can feel like proof of existence. When I was younger, I would make myself bleed just to feel something. I'm not in that place anymore, but the impulse remains—the need to confirm I'm still alive, still real, still here.

Where I Am With This:

The closing verses acknowledge the cyclical nature. And when the silence pulls me back, I'll crave the pain I thought I lacked. There's no resolution, no breaking free. I know I'll return to these empty fixes. Almost alive, just for tonight is the most I can hope for. The desperate clinging to one last breath before the light suggests someone maintaining minimal function, using whatever stimulus they can find to stay marginally engaged with existence. It's survival, but a grim version—just preventing complete dissolution through repeated jolts to a system that's otherwise shut down.

Waiting For More

I walk along the scaffolding in my mind,
Every vision ahead is one I hope to find.
A fleeting glow in a shadowed place,
Moments pass, but I can't embrace.

Chasing glimpses that promise a thrill,
Shiny things and dreams to fill.
The rush arrives, then slips away,
Hunger lingers where joy should stay.
Plans stacked high, horizons just out of reach,
I'm living for the next wave, the next beach.
Tomorrow's hope is what keeps me alive,
Today feels hollow, but I still survive.
Counting moments like footsteps in the sand,
Every step forward, a map in my hand.
The build keeps moving, I can't stand still,
Chasing something I never will.

I'm always moving, afraid to pause,
Each fleeting thrill another cause.
Life lifts me higher, yet I barely land,
Grasping at clouds with an empty hand.

I'm reaching out for something I can feel,
A future light to make the hollow real.
Plans and visions, rising just ahead,
A path to follow, a thread to thread.

Every thrill arrives with a heartbeat quick,
Every moment new, another flick.
The rush of progress, then emptiness hits,
The present fades while my mind commits.
Shadows stretch along the road I tread,
Moments climbing while today lies dead.
If I pause now, will the air collapse?
So I move forward, filling empty gaps.
Even joy comes with a fleeting sigh,
A brief sunbeam before it leaves the sky.

Yet still I chase, I plan, I yearn,
For glimpses tomorrow that may not return.

I live on scaffolding, afraid to stand,
Happiness slips right through my hands.
The moment fades, the plans remain,
I chase the light, I chase the flame.

I'm reaching out for something I can feel,
A future light to make the hollow real.
Plans and visions, rising just ahead,
A path to follow, a thread to thread.

The horizon stretches far above,
Tomorrow's promise is all I love.
I move, I plan, I climb, I strive,
Always forward, barely alive.

Song Summary:
The compulsion to always have something to look forward to—vacations, projects, purchases—using tomorrow's promise as a shield against stopping long enough to think about all the bad things in life.

What I Was Actually Writing About:
When the little releases like a sugary beverage no longer do it for me, I look for the bigger things like an upcoming vacation or home improvement project. I fear that if I have nothing to look forward to I will stop and think for too long. When I stop and think I'll think about all the bad things in my life and I'll get deeper into depression. It's an unhealthy approach, but it's what I deal with. I construct an endless succession of anticipated events—purchases, trips, milestones—using tomorrow's promise as a shield against today's emptiness. I exist not in the moment but on scaffolding, always building toward the next thing, terrified of what might surface if I ever stopped planning and simply inhabited the present. The central compulsion is using anticipation as emotional scaffolding. Tomorrow's hope is what keeps me alive. Today feels hollow, but I still survive. I can only tolerate the present by focusing on future rewards. Each goal provides temporary motivation, but once achieved, it fails to deliver lasting satisfaction.

The Pattern/Mechanism:
This creates an addictive cycle where fulfillment always exists just beyond reach, requiring constant generation of new targets to maintain forward motion. The imagery of scaffolding perfectly captures the precariousness—temporary structures meant to support building something permanent, but in this case, the scaffolding has become the permanent state. I live on scaffolding, afraid to stand. Happiness slips right through my hands. I recognize I'm not actually building toward anything; I'm just maintaining perpetual forward motion to avoid collapse. Nothing can compete with the idealized version that existed in anticipation. Even joy comes with a fleeting sigh. A brief sunbeam before it leaves the sky.

The Tension:

Profound fear underlies this pattern. If I pause now, will the air collapse? Standing still feels dangerous, like it might expose me to the dark thoughts I'm desperately outrunning. The constant planning and anticipation serve as distraction, keeping my mind occupied with logistics and fantasy rather than allowing it to settle into potentially threatening stillness. I'm always moving, afraid to pause because stopping means confronting whatever lies beneath the activity. There's poignant awareness of what this costs. Moments pass, but I can't embrace them. Life happens in the present, but I'm psychologically absent, always living in projected future states. My kids are growing up and I'm missing it because I'm always focused on the next thing.

Where I Am With This:

The closing lines acknowledge the trap without escape: The horizon stretches far above. Tomorrow's promise is all I love. I move, I plan, I climb, I strive. Always forward, barely alive. This isn't living but rather an elaborate avoidance mechanism—using the future as a drug to numb the present, maintaining the cycle because stopping feels impossibly dangerous.

Was it Worth it?

I trace the lines that led me here,
The choices made, the cost unclear.
Moments linger, pulse within my chest,
I wonder if I chose the path that's best.

Could I have taken roads unknown?
Built a life in ways I've never shown?
Every twist and turn, every fork I passed,
Leaves me thinking, did I move too fast?
The victories feel heavy, the wins feel thin,
Every triumph carries the weight within.
I second-guess the moments I believed,
And all the lessons I've yet to perceive.
What if the detours held the key?
Would I have found more clarity?
The choices linger, but I press on still,
Learning slowly, shaping my own will.

Whispers of "maybe" float through my mind,
Strings of "what if" I can't leave behind.
But every misstep, every fall I've known,
Built the heart that's standing alone.

Was it worth it, the paths I took?
Every chapter, every closed book.
I question the past, yet I still move on,
Lessons learned, though some are gone.
Was it worth it, the choices made?
Every shadow, every path I paved.
I hold the pieces, I face the night,
Searching for meaning in the fading light.

The roads not taken, they murmur still,
In the quiet moments, they bend my will.
I chase the traces of what could've been,
But the present calls, and I step in.
Every regret a blow, a lesson to find,
Every decision a weight in the mind.

I weigh the losses, I weigh the gain,
I build from the pain, I break from the chain.
The past is a mirror, it shows the way,
Guiding tomorrow from yesterday.
I take a breath, I face the storm,
Learning the patterns, breaking the norm.

Perhaps the path is never wrong,
Each choice a note in life's long song.
Even in doubt, I take the stride,
Trusting the lessons I find inside.

Was it worth it, the roads I walked?
Every silence, every time I talked.
I question the past, yet I still move on,
Lessons learned, though some are gone.
Was it worth it, the choices made?
Every shadow, every path I paved.
I hold the pieces, I face the night,
Searching for meaning in the fading light.

Song Summary:
The exhausting habit of retrospective analysis, constantly auditing life decisions and questioning whether the choices that led here were correct.

What I Was Actually Writing About:
This one is all about retroactive thinking where I analyze my decisions and wonder if I had done things differently would I be in a better place. I try to not live with regrets, I look at them like learning opportunities instead. "Had I done this instead of that, I would be here." Or "I need to consider this next time when I make a decision." It's always analyzing, always refining my internal algorithms to be as fine-tuned as possible. I constantly audit my life decisions and question whether the choices that led here were correct. Rather than accepting the path taken, I compulsively replay forks in the road, wondering if alternative routes might have delivered better outcomes. Even achievements feel uncertain, filtered through the lens of what might have been. I'm haunted by the ghost of alternative lives, parallel versions of myself that made different choices. I second-guess the moments I believed. This transforms accomplishments into ambiguous outcomes.

The Pattern/Mechanism:
This constant questioning undermines present stability. What if the detours held the key? Would I have found more clarity? I can't simply inhabit my current life because I'm perpetually measuring it against imagined alternatives. Forward movement continues but without confidence, always shadowed by doubt. Whispers of "maybe" float through my mind. Strings of "what if" I can't leave behind. The recurring question "Was it worth it?" applied to the paths I took, the choices made, the roads I walked reveals how comprehensively I second-guess my life. Nothing is exempt from this scrutiny. I hold the pieces, I face the night, searching for meaning in the fading light.

The Tension:
There's an attempt to extract meaning from this pattern. Every misstep, every fall I've known, built the heart that's standing alone. I try to reframe past difficulties as necessary formation. Every regret

a blow, a lesson to find. Yet this philosophical reframing doesn't fully silence the questioning. I know I may never arrive at definitive answers but I can't stop seeking them. It's always analyzing, always refining my internal algorithms to be as fine-tuned as possible. I look at them like learning opportunities instead of regrets. But the constant retrospection means I'm never fully at peace with where I am.

Where I Am With This:

The closing offers tentative acceptance without resolution. Perhaps the path is never wrong. Each choice a note in life's long song. The binary of right/wrong choices might be false. All decisions contribute to a larger pattern. Maybe one day I'll trust that the cumulative effect of my choices has value even when individual decisions seem questionable. Yet the ongoing searching for meaning indicates this remains an active struggle.

Spiral

Thoughts keep racing, I can't slow down,
Every detail spinning, I might drown.
The mind won't rest, it twists and bends,
Chasing every corner, where does it end?

What if I stumble? What if I fall?
Questions echo, I hear them all.
Every choice weighed, every move assessed,
My mind won't stop; it won't let me rest.
I spiral deeper, chasing what-ifs,
Imagining failure in thousand shifts.
Plans in my head, perfectly aligned,
But one thought slips, and I'm confined.
I second-guess each step I take,
Every move calculated, a fragile stake.
Sleep escapes me, the hours bleed,
My thoughts demand, my mind won't heed.

Caught in loops that twist and wind,
Shadows I chase, clarity confined.
The weight of "what if" pulls me down,
I fight for footing, yet might drown.

I'm trapped in my mind, spinning so fast,
Every detail questioned, nothing will last.
Tension rises, the current flows,
I fight the spiral, but the chaos grows.
I fight the spiral, I fight the fear,
Can I find my footing while the end is near?

Check and recheck, the cycle spins,
Every flaw amplified, every doubt begins.
The rabbit holes dig, the walls press in,
I chase the answers I can't ever win.
Every fear magnified, every risk exposed,
I try to rest, but the mind's enclosed.
If I fail, if I can't, if I break the line,
The thoughts scream louder, I'm out of time.

Yet even in chaos, I push through,
Each step forward, though vision's skewed.
Paralyzed by doubt, yet I keep the pace,
Trying to escape the spiral's embrace.

Maybe the spiral is a test I face,
A storm of the mind I must embrace.
Even in fear, I take one stride,
Holding my ground, though worlds collide.

I'm trapped in my mind, spinning so fast,
Every detail questioned, nothing will last.
Tension rises, the current flows,
I fight the spiral, but the chaos grows.
I fight the spiral, I fight the fear,
Can I find my footing while the end is near?

The thoughts slow down, but never cease,
I find some calm, a fleeting peace.
One step forward, the spiral remains,
But I keep moving through the mental chains.

Song Summary:
The visceral experience of obsessive overthinking where the mind becomes a trap of its own making, unable to escape analysis paralysis.

What I Was Actually Writing About:
This takes that Was it Worth it and turns it up a notch. This one is all about how I end up in these thought spirals about over analyzing and over thinking. I can't stop my mind from going down random rabbit holes that don't need to be considered. I exist in relentless mental motion—analyzing, predicting, catastrophizing—unable to slow the torrent of thoughts that circle endlessly without resolution. The central torment is the inability to escape analysis paralysis. Every decision triggers exhaustive examination of potential outcomes. I don't simply make choices and move forward; each option spawns cascading scenarios that must be mentally rehearsed and evaluated. This hypervigilance treats every minor decision as critically important, loading mundane moments with unbearable significance.

The Pattern/Mechanism:
Overthinking creates its own captivity. I spiral deeper, chasing what-ifs, imagining failure in thousand shifts. My mind becomes a simulation machine running endless worst-case scenarios, none of which may materialize but all feel urgently real. This mental churning doesn't produce clarity or solutions; it generates more questions, more angles to consider, more potential disasters to prevent. Plans in my head, perfectly aligned, but one thought slips, and I'm confined. Trapped in my mind, spinning so fast. Caught in loops that twist and wind. It's not linear problem-solving but circular rumination that returns to the same fears from different angles. The rabbit holes dig, the walls press in. The more I think, the more constrained I feel, as if analysis itself is constructing the prison.

The Tension:
Physical manifestation: Sleep escapes me, the hours bleed. The overthinking invades rest, making relaxation impossible. Check and recheck, the cycle spins. Compulsive verification behaviors emerge as I try to manage anxiety through control, but this only feeds the

112

spiral. My mind demands constant attention, won't let me rest, creating exhaustion without relief. Yet even within chaos, I push through. Each step forward, though vision's skewed. I don't stop functioning, but operate while cognitively compromised. This takes "Was it Worth it" and turns it up several notches. I end up in these thought spirals about over analyzing and over thinking. I can't stop my mind from going down random rabbit holes that don't need to be considered.

Where I Am With This:
The closing suggests the spiral never fully resolves. The thoughts slow down, but never cease. I find some calm, a fleeting peace. There are moments of reduced intensity, but the underlying pattern persists. One step forward, the spiral remains. This isn't triumph over the spiral but rather adaptation to its permanent presence.

Still Standing

I don't know how I'm still here,
Bones ache, but the path stays clear.
Every scar a map I can't erase,
Still breathing, still keeping pace.

Every night I collapse, but the morning pulls me,
Gravity heavy, but something still fuels me.
Been through fires that hollowed my chest,
Learned to keep moving, never learned rest.
Hands still shake from the weight I hold,
Carried too much, turned flesh to mold.
Lesser souls turned ghosts in my lane,
But I keep walking through smoke and pain.
I forgot how to stop, forgot what peace means,
Body's on autopilot, heart runs routines.
Even silence hums like it's keeping score,
I've been breaking for years, but I'm asking for more.

How am I still standing tall,
When I should've crumbled after it all?
No rest, no cure, no proof,
Just steps that keep moving through truth.

Still standing, though I've fallen inside,
Still moving through the pain I hide.
Don't ask how, I don't know why,
I just breathe, I just survive.

My reflection stares like it don't belong,
Eyes like glass, but the will stays strong.
I've buried versions of me that quit,
Each grave a lesson I won't forget.
The body remembers what the mind lets go,
The ache, the weight, the undertow.
Still I walk, still I bleed in time,
Pain's the rhythm, and the beat's still mine.
They call it strength — I call it fear,
A refusal to stop, to disappear.

I've lost so much I forgot what's due,
But somehow I keep coming through.

Even I can't explain the motion,
Moving through fire like it's ocean.
Cracked and worn, but not confined —
Somehow the pieces still align.

Still standing, though I've fallen inside,
Still moving through the pain I hide.
Don't ask how, I don't know why,
I just breathe, I just survive.

If I stop now, I might not start,
But motion's all that shields my heart.
Still standing, still alive,
Barely here, but I survive.

Song Summary:
Hard-won recognition of resilience—despite everything that should have broken me, I remain, bewildered by survival that defies my own understanding.

What I Was Actually Writing About:
One of my biggest fantasies is to walk into a doctor's office and for the doctor to be like, "How are you still functioning?" To be in complete awe with my ability to keep standing after everything I've endured. I feel like I've been through hell and back in my life and sometimes I'm amazed that I'm still here, that I'm still where I am today. I have a good job, I have a nice house, I have a loving wife and kids. But how do I have these things when I'm as broken as I am? I don't know how I'm still here. This isn't triumphant celebration but bewildered acknowledgment of survival that defies my own understanding. I've absorbed damage that hollowed my chest, carried weight that turned flesh to mold, walked through fires that destroyed others—yet somehow continue functioning. There's almost defiant confusion: How am I still standing tall, when I should've crumbled after it all? The survival itself becomes the achievement.

The Pattern/Mechanism:
The cost: I forgot how to stop, forgot what peace means. Body's on autopilot, heart runs routines. I haven't thrived so much as automated survival, becoming a machine of persistence. Hands still shake from the weight I hold. The standing isn't graceful; it's scarred, exhausted, operating on momentum rather than vitality. My reflection stares like it don't belong. Eyes like glass, but the will stays strong. Disconnection between the battered vessel and the stubborn force that keeps it moving. I've buried versions of me that quit. Each grave a lesson I won't forget. The current standing self is a series of reconstructions, phoenix-like rises from previous collapses. The body remembers what the mind lets go. Trauma lives in physical memory even when cognitively processed.

The Tension:
There's complexity in how I interpret my own resilience. They call it strength—I call it fear. A refusal to stop, to disappear. This

116

reframes endurance not as heroic choice but as inability to surrender, a terror of cessation that propels forward motion even when rest might be more appropriate. I've lost so much I forgot what's due. The closing captures ambiguous victory: Still standing, still alive. Barely here, but I survive. This isn't about flourishing but the bare minimum of continued existence. If I stop now, I might not start. The standing is maintained through fear of what stopping might mean, suggesting fragility beneath the resilience. One of my biggest fantasies is walking into a doctor's office and having them marvel at how I'm still functioning.

Where I Am With This:

Yet there's genuine amazement: Even I can't explain the motion. My own survival exceeds my rational understanding. The song doesn't resolve into confidence or peace, but it offers a moment of recognition—however damaged, however uncertain, however exhausted, I remain standing, and that itself is worth noting.

Trained For This

I've walked these roads, each step a weight,
Every scar and shadow built this state.
The nights were long, the fires deep,
But here I stand, awake from sleep.

The road was crooked, the paths were sharp,
Lessons etched in every mark.
Pain taught me patience, loss taught me drive,
Every fall was a reason to survive.
I've carried doubts that would crush most men,
But I learned to rise again and again.
Every choice, every wrong, every fear I kissed,
Prepared me for this — I was trained for this.
No moment wasted, no lesson gone,
Each heartbreak a forge where I became strong.
I walk forward knowing what I've earned,
Every mile behind me, every corner turned.

The wind bites, but my pace holds firm,
Every stumble is a silent term.
I've been hardened by the fire, the storm, the fight,
And every shadow only fuels my light.

I was trained for this, every scar, every fall,
Every step I've taken answers the call.
The path is hard, but I know my way,
I endure, I persist, I continue today.

I've worn the weight like armor thick,
Lessons pressed into every nick.
The pain I faced was the sculptor's hand,
Shaping my will to finally stand.
I've seen the nights where hope grew thin,
Felt the storm rage deep within.
But each trial became a rhythm, a beat,
Every heartbeat training my resolve, my feat.
No turning back, no shortcuts found,
The grind of life has my soul bound.

And though the road is endless, I persist,
Every step forward — proof I exist.

Every lesson carried, every wound I know,
I've learned the hard way, but I'm still whole.
Each challenge faced has shaped my way,
And I keep moving, day by day.

I was trained for this, every scar, every fall,
Every step I've taken answers the call.
The path is hard, but I know my way,
I endure, I persist, I continue today.

The road stretches on, I take my stride,
Every choice behind me, nothing to hide.
I've learned from the fire, the storm, the fight,
Each step I take carries my might.
The weight I bear has made me whole,
Forward I move, guided by my soul.

Song Summary:
Transforming accumulated suffering into armor and expertise, reframing past pain as rigorous preparation that created someone purpose-built for adversity.

What I Was Actually Writing About:
I feel like with all of the issues that I've faced in my life, even though I'm emotionally numb to so many different things, I know I can withstand most issues that come my way. I feel like I've been trained for hardship, forged in fire. I look at all the hardships and see that little things that other people would complain about, I see as a minimal issue and I can overcome it, I've been through worse, I've endured harder times. This is nothing. Where "Still Standing" expressed bewildered survival, "Trained For This" claims intentional readiness. Every trial, every scar is reinterpreted not as random damage but as curriculum in an unintentional education for resilience. The central assertion: pain has been formative rather than merely destructive. The wounds aren't just marks of what was endured but building blocks of current strength. Suffering becomes pedagogy, each difficulty imparting specific lessons that accumulate into comprehensive readiness.

The Pattern/Mechanism:
Hard-earned confidence absent from earlier songs. I walk forward knowing what I've earned. Every mile behind me, every corner turned. There's ownership of the journey and pride in having traversed it. I no longer question whether I'm capable; my past provides empirical evidence of capacity. I've carried doubts that would crush most men, but I learned to rise again and again. This isn't theoretical self-belief but confidence rooted in documented survival. The recurring declaration "I was trained for this" functions as both mantra and truth claim. Whatever challenge arrives next, I've already encountered analogous difficulty and learned how to endure. Every step I've taken answers the call. Past struggles created someone purpose-built for adversity.

The Tension:
Acknowledgment that this training was brutal. I've been hardened by the fire, the storm, the fight. The process wasn't gentle but violent

forging. Lessons pressed into every nick. The grind of life has my soul bound. The education came at tremendous cost, left permanent marks. I've worn the weight like armor thick suggests both protection gained and burden that never fully lifts. The path is hard, but I know my way. Hardship isn't shocking anymore; it's familiar terrain I've learned to navigate. I look at all the hardships and see that little things that other people would complain about, I see as a minimal issue. I've been through worse. I've endured harder times. This is nothing.

Where I Am With This:
The poem doesn't claim the journey is complete. The road stretches on, I take my stride. Each step I take carries my might. Where earlier songs documented feeling overwhelmed or barely surviving, this piece claims mastery earned through suffering. The weight I bear has made me whole. Forward I move, guided by my soul. The same experiences that could have destroyed me have instead created completeness—trained, prepared, and ready for whatever comes next.

Collection III

My Demons

This is the collection I buried for years. It's easier to write about symptoms than to name their source. Easier to document struggles than to point at the person who caused them. Easier to claim strength through survival than to admit what you had to survive. This is about excavating the trauma I've spent a lifetime trying to contain—about giving voice to the demons that shaped me, controlled me, and nearly destroyed me before I learned to lock them away.

What This Collection Is

This collection descends into the origin. It names the abuse explicitly — not "difficult childhood" but specific acts of violence, control, abandonment, and psychological torture. It traces how family trauma spread into romantic relationships, how you can physically escape an abuser but carry their voice in your head for decades, how trauma doesn't just hurt you — it threatens to erase you entirely.

The structure mirrors trauma's actual progression: burial (denial), eruption (crisis), escape (hope), return (reality), and finally control (management). Not healing. Not redemption. Not forgiveness. Just hard-won dominance over internal forces that once dominated me.

This is the collection that explains everything that came before. Why I can't trust. Why I hyperplan. Why I see the monster in the mirror. Why I'm exhausted. Why connection feels dangerous. Why I had to become strong enough to survive alone.

Unlike Collection I's movement toward vulnerable connection or Collection II's claiming of solitary resilience, Collection III descends into the source of all previous suffering, names it explicitly, then charts a path not to healing but to management — transforming from being controlled by demons to controlling them.

Key Themes

Trauma as Living Entity: The buried pain didn't stay buried—it animated, developed agency, became demons that pace and whisper and claw. Every coping strategy I developed (documented in Collections I & II) was a response to these internal presences that know me intimately because they are me—the parts I tried to reject, the survival mechanisms that became prisons.

The Architecture of Abuse: This collection maps the system precisely. My father's explosive violence created baseline terror. My mother's abandonment eliminated any protective buffer and later denied my reality. My father's total control suppressed autonomous self-development. Punishment for resistance taught helplessness. Impossible standards installed internal tyranny. Together, these created comprehensive machinery designed to break a child's spirit.

Seeing the Abuser in Myself: I don't just remember the abuse—I carry it. His rage in my rage. His control in my control. The traits I most despise appearing in my own face, my own reactions. This is the nightmare: that I can't escape him because he's written into me, genetic or learned or both, inescapable.

The Spread of Trauma: Abuse doesn't stay confined. Childhood wounds made me vulnerable to toxic romantic relationships— unable to recognize manipulation as abnormal, trained to accept harm as a component of love, desperate for care in ways that made me exploitable. The poison entered through wounds that were already open.

The Inadequacy of Physical Escape: Military service gave me distance, structure, chosen family, first experience of agency—all genuinely life-saving. But the demons traveled because they're internalized. I can change geography without changing the neural pathways carved by years of terror. The house of wrath isn't a place I left—it's internal architecture.

The Question of Self: After documenting all this damage, I arrive at the existential crisis: Do I even exist as a coherent person? Or am I just a collection of trauma responses pretending to be human? Has trauma destroyed who I might have been, or revealed who I actually am? This is the nadir—the moment where accumulated damage threatens to erase any authentic self.

Control, Not Cure: The resolution isn't healing. It's transformation from being controlled by demons to controlling them. I become the warden of my own internal prison. The demons still live in the halls—they always will. But I hold the keys. I decide when doors open. I feed them measured rations rather than letting them feed freely on my fear.

Why I Wrote This

I didn't want to write this collection. I spent years burying these memories, these demons, because looking at them directly felt too dangerous. The abuse happened decades ago. Why couldn't I just move on? Why did it still matter?

But the demons don't stay buried. They claw their way up. They whisper in quiet moments. They shape every relationship, every choice, every moment of trust or mistrust. You can try to outrun them, but they're not external—they're you. The terrified child still living in your nervous system. The survival mechanisms that won't turn off. The voice of the abuser that you've internalized so completely you can't distinguish it from your own thoughts.

Writing these poems meant going back to the house of wrath. It meant naming my father's violence and my mother's abandonment explicitly. It meant admitting that toxic relationships exploited vulnerabilities I didn't know I had. It meant confronting the possibility that trauma didn't just damage me—it might have erased whoever I was supposed to be.

The hardest part wasn't the pain. Pain I could handle. The hardest part was the question "Is This Me?" The moment of looking at myself and genuinely not knowing if there was an authentic self underneath all the trauma responses, or if trauma was all there was.

But I also had to write the ending honestly. I didn't heal. I didn't forgive. I didn't transcend. What I did was claim control. I became for myself what I needed as a child: a protective authority figure who establishes boundaries, maintains safety, refuses to let harmful forces dominate. The demons still live in the halls. But I'm the warden now. And that—however cold, however difficult—is freedom of a kind.

The Emotional Journey

This collection operates primarily in registers of horror, rage, grief, and eventual grim determination. The opening songs carry visceral dread—the feeling of something dangerous stirring in darkness. The middle songs documenting specific abuse burn with fury—at my father's violence, at my mother's abandonment, at the systems that failed to protect a child. There's profound sorrow for the childhood lost, the self that never got to develop, the years spent in survival mode rather than growth.

Shame threads through heavily—wrestling with how I've been changed by abuse, how I may have absorbed and replicated toxic patterns, whether I've become the very thing that hurt me. This shame is more corrosive than the earlier collections' self-doubt because it questions fundamental worth and nature.

"Run Free" introduces exhilaration and hope—rare emotions in these collections—the rush of escape and discovery that another way of living exists. But "Whispers Return" tempers this with exhausted recognition that the fight isn't over, can't be over, will require ongoing effort.

The final piece achieves something like cold satisfaction—not happiness or peace but the grim pleasure of having seized control, of having transformed from powerless child to empowered adult, of having claimed authority over internal landscape.

The Arc

Where it starts: "Buried Deep"—the demons I tried to contain are stirring, clawing, demanding recognition. The strategy of suppression is failing.

Where it descends: The specific traumas. "House of Wrath"—my father's violence and learning to read danger in floorboards. "The Fallen Beacon"—my mother's abandonment and denial. "Marionette"—total control that prevented autonomous self. "The Quicksand Wins"—punishment for resistance. "Summit and Storm"—impossible standards that never end.

Where it spreads: "The Poison Bloom"—how childhood wounds made me vulnerable to toxic romantic relationships that fed on my damage.

Where I dissolve: "Is This Me?"—existential crisis. Looking at myself and genuinely questioning whether any authentic person survived, or if I'm just trauma responses pretending to be human.

Where I escape: "Run Free"—military service providing distance, structure, chosen family. First experience of agency and self-determination. The exhilaration of breaking chains.

Where reality hits: "Whispers Return"—discovering that physical escape isn't enough. The demons traveled with me because they're internalized. Geography changed but the architecture remained.

Where I arrive: "Control"—transformation from victim of internal voices to warden of them. The demons still exist, still whisper, still claw. But now they operate under my authority. I hold the keys. I decide when doors open. I feed them measured rations. They're part of me—acknowledged, contained, managed.

This collection argues that management is a valid endpoint, not a waystation to something better. For some trauma survivors, the best achievable outcome isn't peace or healing but stable functioning through disciplined containment of psychological damage.

The demons live in the halls. They always will. But I hold the keys. And sometimes — after everything — that's enough.

Content Warning

Read this carefully before proceeding.

This collection contains explicit, detailed descriptions of:

- **Childhood physical abuse**: A father's unpredictable violence, children learning to read environmental cues for danger, living in sustained terror
- **Parental abandonment**: A mother who strategically absented herself during abuse and later denied it happened, rewriting history to absolve herself
- **Psychological control**: Total domination of a child's autonomy, suppression of independent self, impossible standards, punishment for resistance
- **Toxic romantic relationships**: Exploitation of trauma-created vulnerabilities, manipulation disguised as love
- **Existential dissolution**: Questioning whether any authentic self survived the abuse, suicidal ideation
- **Rage**: Visceral, explicit anger at abusers

The tone moves from horror (stirring demons) through fury (naming the abuse) to grief (mourning who I might have been) to cold determination (claiming control).

This is the hardest collection to read. If you're a trauma survivor, some of these poems may be triggering. If you need to stop, stop. If you need to skip pieces, skip them. If you need to come back later, come back later. Your safety matters more than finishing a book.

Buried Deep

I buried them in the depths of my chest
Thought the darkness would put them to rest
Whispers crawling, calling out my name
In the silence, nothing feels the same

They pace my mind, I feel them in the night
Claws of memory digging, claws I cannot fight
Eyes in the corners, watching as I breathe
Voices in the static, never let me leave
They echo my thoughts, they finish my lines
A chorus of ghosts in the back of my mind
I've locked them away, but they learned to survive
Creeping through my dreams, keeping me alive
I hear them whisper when the lights go dim
Footsteps in my head, singing their hymn
I can't outrun them, they know where I hide
Every heartbeat trembles when they come inside
Hardened by fear, but still I feel the chill
Their whispers pierce silence, bending iron will
I thought I could cage them, thought I could rest
But the demons remember, they know me best

Can you hear them scratching beneath your skin?
Breathing heavy, leaving nothing within
They stir, they whisper, they need to be freed
And I'm trembling under what they breed

Demons awake, they won't let me sleep
Haunting my thoughts, crawling in deep
If you saw them staring through my eyes
Would you stay, or would you despise?
They whisper secrets I can't contain
Sharp as knives, soaked in pain
Demons awake, tearing at the night
I hold my love close, but they bite

I feel their breath against my skin
Every hidden fear, every sin

Demons that scream, demons that leer
Every step I take, they're always near
I've trained my heart to mask the dread
But every word I speak is haunted, unsaid
Your eyes on me, would you even see
The monsters I fight that will never flee?
I've let them dance in the corners of my mind
Hoping to keep their hunger confined
But they claw and whisper, they want it all
And every quiet moment, I fear their call
I'm digging inside, confronting what I dread
Hoping my soul doesn't break instead

They were never gone, just lurking inside
Eyes in the dark where I cannot hide
Facing them burns, but I cannot flee
And still, I wonder if you'll stay with me

Demons awake, they claw and they rise
No more hiding, no more lies
If you saw the darkness I hold inside
Would you stay, or would you divide?
They whisper my name, they tear at the night
I fight to keep you safe in their sight
Demons awake, relentless and real
But in your love, maybe I can heal

They're clawing the walls, they're breaking the floor
Voices I buried are louder than before
The ground is shaking, the air turns cold
They're coming for the secrets I've tried to hold
I can hear them rising, they're pulling me down
The demons I buried have taken the crown

Song Summary:
Internalized trauma as living entities that cannot be destroyed, only contained—demons deliberately buried that refuse to stay dormant.

What I Was Actually Writing About:
This one is all about how all the issues from my youth have been buried deep inside of me. I don't talk about these things because they're hard, they don't come up in conversations organically, and quite frankly they're past events that I just want to forget about. But these events are part of who I am today. I describe burying my emotional wounds and psychological pain—placing them "in the depths of my chest." But these buried elements refuse to stay dormant; they've taken on a life of their own, becoming "demons" that pace, whisper, and claw at the walls of their confinement. The central horror is that suppression doesn't eliminate—it animates. I believed that pushing pain down deep enough would neutralize it, but instead the buried emotions have become active presences.

The Pattern/Mechanism:
The song reveals how these buried demons have become intimate companions despite—or because of—their containment. They echo my thoughts, they finish my lines, a chorus of ghosts in the back of my mind—I can't distinguish between my own voice and the voices of suppressed trauma. The demons know me completely: they know where I hide, they know me best. This creates unsettling intimacy where the most threatening presences are also the most familiar, the parts of self that have been rejected but remain inextricably bound. There's escalating tension as the song progresses. I hear them whisper when the lights go dim, footsteps in my head, singing their hymn—the demons become more vocal in vulnerable moments, darkness and quiet allowing them prominence.

The Tension:
The refrain "Demons awake" signals crisis point. What was buried is rising, what was locked away is clawing and tearing at the night. I recognize I can't outrun them, that my strategy of suppression has failed catastrophically. Yet there's also acknowledgment that these demons are part of self: They were never gone, just lurking inside. The buried material is revealed not as external threat but as rejected

aspects of my own psyche demanding recognition. I don't talk about these things because they're hard, they don't come up in conversations organically, and quite frankly they're past events that I just want to forget about. But these events are part of who I am today.

Where I Am With This:
When I started writing these songs, I found the most personal, meaningful ones were the most traumatic. I'm trying to control these suppressed feelings by giving them space in lyrics.

House of Wrath

The air would freeze before the storm,
A quiet threat that took its form.
We'd hold our breath, afraid to move,
The wind would shift — we always knew.

The ground would shake before the rain,
Each tremor humming with old pain.
Walls would sigh, the lights would dim,
The air grew sharp — we'd hide within.
The house would groan, the demons learned,
To watch us flinch as silence burned.
We read the room through floorboard creaks,
The sound of wrath beneath our feet.
Two hearts running through the yard of night,
Carrying fear like stolen light.
The grass was wet, the moon would hide,
We prayed the storm would pass us by.
The world stood still, our lungs would ache,
A breath too loud could make us break.
That silence cut, that dread would bloom,
And every shadow filled the room.

Can you hear it echo through the halls?
The sound that makes the sunlight fall.
It hums, it waits, it shakes the floor —
The wrath returns, like once before.

There's no escape, you cannot hide,
The walls are watching from inside.
Make no sound, keep tearless eyes,
The silence screams, the truth denies.
The air is thick, the fear alive,
This house of wrath will not subside.

We spoke in whispers, soft and small,
Afraid our words would shake the wall.
The rooms could hear, they seemed alive,
Breathing the fear we'd try to hide.

We built our peace from fleeting things,
Like birds that fly with broken wings.
The night would hum, the air would change,
That same old dread, familiar pain.
Years have passed, the echoes stay,
In the way I flinch, the things I say.
A grown man now, but I still feel,
That low vibration — sharp, unreal.
The storm still knocks, though it's long gone,
It hums beneath my every song.

The house still stands, though the rooms are bare,
The walls remember, they always stare.
I walk the halls with steady breath,
But the floor still creaks with what was left.

There's no escape, you cannot hide,
The ghosts you fear now live inside.
Make no sound, keep tearless eyes,
The storm still hums beneath your lies.
The thunder fades, the air goes dry,
But the house of wrath will never die.

The walls still breathe, the air still tight,
The floorboards whisper through the night.
I tell myself the storm is gone,
But the house still hums — it's never done.

Song Summary:
Childhood lived under the constant threat of paternal violence, where survival required perpetual hypervigilance and reading every environmental cue.

What I Was Actually Writing About:
My father was an abusive man. When he would come home from a long day of manual labor and the chores weren't done, or done to his level of satisfaction, we'd get the belt. If we said something that he thought was back talk, we'd get the belt. It was such a frequent event that me and one of my brothers would always sneak out the back door when we heard his truck roll into the driveway, afraid that he would be in one of his bad moods. My brother and I existed in a state of perpetual hypervigilance, learning to read environmental cues that signaled impending abuse. The central experience is living with unpredictable rage. We learned absolute stillness, making ourselves small and silent to avoid triggering our father's wrath. The house itself becomes animate with threat—walls sighing, lights dimming, the house groaning, floorboard creaks carrying messages of danger. This reveals how thoroughly our senses became attuned to our environment.

The Pattern/Mechanism:
The song captures the terror of anticipatory fear. We read the room through floorboard creaks, the sound of wrath beneath our feet—the abuse wasn't constant but its possibility was, creating sustained dread perhaps more damaging than the violence itself. That silence cut, that dread would bloom, and every shadow filled the room. The waiting, the knowing it was coming but not when, trained us into states of chronic activation where relaxation became impossible. The refrain "There's no escape, you cannot hide, the walls are watching from inside" captures the totality of entrapment. This wasn't abuse we could physically flee—we lived within it, depended on our abuser for survival, had nowhere safe to go. The instruction "Make no sound, keep tearless eyes" reveals the rules we learned: suppress all emotional expression, show no weakness, give no reaction that might escalate violence.

The Tension:

The song's most powerful element is its revelation of permanence: Years have passed, the echoes stay. I'm now a grown man physically removed from the childhood home, yet I still feel that low vibration—sharp, unreal. The hypervigilance never turned off. I walk the halls with steady breath, but the floor still creaks with what was left. When my father would come home from work and the chores weren't done to his satisfaction, we'd get the belt. It was such a frequent event that my brother and I would sneak out the back door when we heard his truck roll into the driveway, afraid that he would be in one of his bad moods.

Where I Am With This:

I now sit with this uncomfortable feeling that something is always coming and I need to be hypervigilant. The danger has passed, but my body doesn't know that. I still hear the truck in the driveway, still prepare to run, still can't fully relax.

Fallen Beacon

The tide would crash against the stone,
You stood above, a light once shown.
But somewhere lost between the gray,
The beacon dimmed, it turned away.

The wind would howl, the night would cry,
The sea would mirror every lie.
You said the storm would pass, be still,
But thunder knows it always will.
You built your calm from fragile glass,
Pretending not to hear the past.
Each wave that broke, a whispered plea,
We learned the truth beneath the sea.
Your hands once held the fear at bay,
Now silence takes their place each day.
The light was there, but turned aside,
A promise made, but never tried.
The storm still hums, the wind still screams,
And drowns the sound of broken dreams.

The sea remembers every scar,
The cliffs still echo who we are.
You said you'd guide me through the rain,
But left me drifting in the pain.

You were the light that lost its flame,
A fallen beacon was without blame.
The waves crashed hard, they tore the shore,
And I was left to drift once more.
The storm cries out, but there is no light,
Left alone through the stormy night.

I called your name across the tide,
But echoes were the only guide.
You said it wasn't how I saw,
That pain was just a child's flaw.
But lightning doesn't lie, it burns,
And silence teaches what it learns.

You said the dark was never near,
But I still flinch when thunder's here.
The lighthouse turned, the beam went wide,
You faced the sea — we stayed inside.
Each wave, a memory I fight,
Each sound, a ghost that comes at night.
You claimed the storm was never near,
Yet I still drown when I hear fear.

You said the light would always burn,
But some flames die, they don't return.
You turned away, the night stood tall,
And left us anchored through it all.

You were the light that lost its flame,
A fallen beacon was without blame.
The waves crashed hard, they tore the shore,
And I was left to drift once more.
The storm cries out, but there is no light,

Left alone through the stormy night.

Song Summary:

The mother's passive abandonment and strategic absence during moments of terror, followed by denial that any of it occurred.

What I Was Actually Writing About:

With the physical abuse of my father, my mother was supposed to be there to protect us. There are memories where we were told to go to the couch, the final words before we'd get the belt, and we'd see our mother leave the room. As an adult she claims to not remember it being that bad when we were kids, but she would remove herself before she saw what it was like. Yet she also told me about this time when she informed my father that his kids were scared of him. So she remembers us being scared but not why we were scared. It's like she doesn't want to remember because it would make her feel bad. The beacon metaphor captures what a mother should represent: a guiding light, a source of safety in darkness, someone who stands between children and harm. But this beacon "lost its flame," turning away precisely when most needed. The central wound is abandonment disguised as neutrality. The mother wasn't actively harmful, but her withdrawal at critical moments left us defensively exposed. The storm would approach, and instead of providing shelter or intervention, she offered empty reassurance while doing nothing to prevent the violence.

The Pattern/Mechanism:

The song captures the specific pain of chosen blindness. The mother built her calm from fragile glass, pretending not to hear the past — she maintained her own emotional equilibrium by refusing to acknowledge what was happening. This wasn't ignorance but active denial, a decision to not-see in order to not-act. The most devastating revelation comes in my adult life: You said it wasn't how I saw, that pain was just a child's flaw — the mother rewrote history entirely, suggesting we misremembered or exaggerated, that our trauma wasn't real or wasn't significant. The imagery of lighthouse and sea creates powerful metaphor: I called your name across the tide, but echoes were the only guide — in moments of terror, we looked to our mother for rescue, but she had already turned away.

142

The Tension:

The song refuses to excuse this abandonment. You claimed the storm was never near, yet I still drown when I hear fear—the mother's retrospective denial doesn't erase my ongoing trauma responses. The refrain "You were the light that lost its flame, a fallen beacon without blame" captures bitter irony: she claims innocence because she didn't actively harm, but passivity in the face of children being abused is its own culpability. There are memories where we were told to go to the couch, the final words before we'd get the belt, and we'd see our mother leave the room. As an adult she claims to not remember it being that bad. But she would remove herself before she saw what it was like.

Where I Am With This:

I will never do this to my children. I see this as watching my kids do something dangerous and not stepping forward to protect them. To me it's a sign of being a weak parent—the one thing I refuse to become.

Marionette

I feel the bars against my skin,
The chains around me pull me in.
A silent hand that moves my strings,
I'm caught inside what fear still brings.

The lines are drawn, I step in place,
A measured world, a tethered space.
Each choice I make is watched, weighed down,
The clock strikes judgment in this town.
My hands reach out for something true,
But chains constrict — I cannot break through.
A marionette with careful threads,
I speak in nods, not words unsaid.
The fire inside fights for a spark,
But walls surround, and light is dark.
I dream of song beyond the line,
But whispers tell me it's not mine.
Each move I take is shadowed, timed,
My own desires are undermined.
The cage is tight, the floorboards creak,
The self I crave is far from reach.

I feel the chains grip, they pull me tight,
A silent hand I cannot fight.
I stretch my wings but fear remains,
A marionette within these chains.

The cage within won't let me move,
The strings are pulled by hands I did not choose.
I try to dance, but none can see,
The puppet moves to another beat.
The walls close in, the shadows grin,
I fight, I fall, the cage wins.

I trace the bars with trembling hands,
Each note I long for reprimands.
The world outside feels far away,
Yet still I dream of light someday.

Each step I take is calculated,
Each breath reviewed, evaluated.
I watch the others free to choose,
While I still pay for trying to lose.
The marionette inside me shakes,
I long to break, to cut the stakes.
But fear has roots too deep to find,
It holds the self I left behind.
I reach for song, I reach for air,
Yet feel the chains and threads still there.
The cage expands, then pulls me tight,
The silent hand denies the fight.

I see the key, it gleams, it waits,
Behind the wall of rules and fates.
Give me peace, let me hope,
But tethered with a heavy rope.

The cage within won't let me move,
The strings are pulled by hands I did not choose.
I try to dance, but none can see,
The puppet moves to another beat.
The walls close in, the shadows grin,
I fight, I fall, the cage wins.

The bars are cold, the chains remain,
The silent hand still guides my strain.
The marionette, it twitches still,
Inside the cage against my will.

Song Summary:
Psychological control and total domination of agency, where every choice was surveilled and no autonomous self was permitted to exist.

What I Was Actually Writing About:
My father was also a controlling individual. He was not a good athlete but he believed his children could be under his guidance. It was never what we wanted to do, it was what he wanted. When I was in fifth grade I told him I no longer wanted to go out for this sport. He said that if I didn't I would be grounded for the entire year. As a child I didn't think about how difficult that would be to enforce, I just knew that he would enforce it to some degree. So I continued doing something I didn't care about, because the alternative was punishment. I describe my existence as a puppet with visible strings—every choice surveilled, every desire undermined, every movement controlled. This explores the suffocation of having no autonomy to exist. The central metaphor of puppet and puppeteer captures the complete absence of self-determination. Even without physical restraints, I experience my life as imprisoned. This wasn't obvious coercion but insidious control where my father's will replaced my own. I could imagine what I wanted privately but couldn't actualize those desires without permission, approval, or direction from the controlling hand.

The Pattern/Mechanism:
The song reveals how this control operated through judgment and measurement. Each choice I make is watched, weighed down, the clock strikes judgment in this town—nothing escaped evaluation. Every decision became subject to the father's assessment, creating a measured world, a tethered space where spontaneity and authentic preference couldn't exist. My own desires are undermined—even internal wants became suspect, something to be corrected or redirected according to the father's vision. There's profound grief for the unlived life. I dream of song beyond the line, but whispers tell me it's not mine—I had aspirations, preferences, a sense of who I might become, but these were systematically denied. The self I crave is far from reach because that self was never permitted to develop.

The Tension:

The imagery of cage and strings working together creates layered imprisonment: The cage is tight, the floorboards creak—physical space felt constraining, but the real prison was psychological. The marionette inside me shakes, I long to break, to cut the stakes—even now, removed from the father's direct control, I feel the strings, operate as if I'm still being manipulated. The internalized control has outlasted the controller's presence. When I was in fifth grade I told my father I no longer wanted to play this sport. He said that if I didn't I would be grounded for the entire year. So I continued doing something I didn't care about, because the alternative was punishment.

Where I Am With This:

Now I look at what my kids do and I want to encourage them to do what they want. I still feel like I need to switch hobbies every few months because I have the autonomy to do things I never did before. I'm still trying to find what I enjoy.

The Quicksand Wins

I sink beneath the grinding sand,
No hand to hold, no rescue plan.
The grains they bite, they cut, they bind,
I fight, I thrash, no help to find.

Each step I take just pulls me down,
The weight of words I never drown.
I reach, I grasp, but hands are gone,
The tide of judgment drags me on.
I carve my path through coarse terrain,
But nothing I do can break the chain.
The soil grates, it scratches skin,
I strain for life, my lifeline thin.
I kick, I reach, the pull is rough,
The tide of sand says I'm not enough.
Each breath I take is grit and grind,
The noose of failure wraps my mind.
The earth it shifts, it grips, it wins,
I feel the weight beneath my sins.

I reach for hands that aren't there,
I strain, I call, but none can care.
The sand it bites, the pressure stays,
I fight alone through endless days.

I reach, I kick, cannot rise,
The quicksand grips, when I try.
I stretch my arms, but they don't hold,
The quicksand pulls, will not let go.
I fight, I scream, it never ends,
No rescue comes, no hand extends.
The earth consumes, the pull begins,
I thrash, I fall, the quicksand wins.
The quicksand wins.

The harder I push, the faster I slide,
The grains they grind, they won't subside.
Every move judged, every step too slow,

I bend, I break, yet they won't know.
I've tried to carve a different way,
But rules and scorn will always stay.
I stretch for air, my lungs ignite,
Yet still the pressure holds me tight.
The sand scratches, cuts, and binds,
The path I want is hard to find.
No matter the effort, no matter the plea,
The weight persists relentlessly.
Hands that should catch are nowhere near,
The pull of failure is all I hear.
I push, I pull, yet still descend,
The grinding earth will not relent.

I see the surface, faint and far,
A fleeting hope, a distant star.
Give me peace, a chance to stand,
But I'm tethered here, gripped by sand.

I reach, I kick, cannot rise,
The quicksand grips, when I try.
I stretch my arms, but they don't hold,
The quicksand pulls, will not let go.
I fight, I scream, it never ends,
No rescue comes, no hand extends.
The earth consumes, the pull begins,
I thrash, I fall, the quicksand wins.
The quicksand wins.

The sand it grinds, it will not yield,
No hand appears, no open field.
I thrash, I strain, I reach, I spin,
Alone, I sink — the quicksand wins.

Song Summary:
The crushing futility of resistance where every effort to escape or assert independence only pulled deeper into suffocating control.

What I Was Actually Writing About:
One of my brothers had decided to do something rebellious by printing out some song lyrics for a Linkin Park song and taped them to the fridge, a song about control. My father didn't raise his voice, didn't hit anyone, but he did write his own notes on the lyrics, twisting the words to fit his reign in the house. Any effort to say we wanted to do something different was met with futility. When I said I wanted to go out for choir he said, "You're only doing it for a girl." I wasn't supported, I was pushed down and made to feel inferior for wanting to do something else. This captures what happened when we attempted to fight back—discovering that every effort to escape or assert independence only pulled us deeper into suffocating control. The quicksand metaphor conveys how struggle itself became the mechanism of entrapment: the harder you fight, the faster you sink. The central horror is that resistance accelerates subjugation. We were alone in our struggles, with no allies, no intervention, no one to pull us free. Attempts at autonomy, at carving independent path, at escaping our father's control didn't lead toward freedom but deeper into constraint.

The Pattern/Mechanism:
The song reveals the abrasive, punishing nature of this dynamic. The sand doesn't just constrain—it bites, it cuts, it grinds, it scratches skin. This isn't passive containment but active punishment for resistance. Every move judged, every step too slow—the father assessed each action, finding it inadequate, using my efforts as evidence of failure rather than recognizing them as assertion of self. There's devastating absence of support. I reach for hands that aren't there, I strain, I call, but none can care—connecting to "The Fallen Beacon," the mother doesn't intervene. No one pulls me out; no one validates my struggle; no one acknowledges the impossibility of my position.

The Tension:

The physical imagery conveys claustrophobic desperation: I kick, I reach, cannot rise, my lungs ignite, yet still the pressure holds me tight. I'm suffocating under the weight of control that responds to resistance by tightening. Rules and scorn will always stay — no matter what I do, the system remains rigged. The refrain "The quicksand wins" becomes mantra of defeat learned through repeated experience. One of my brothers printed out song lyrics and taped them to the fridge, an act of rebellion. My father wrote his own demeaning notes on them and taped them back to the fridge. Any effort to say we wanted to do something different was met with futility.

Where I Am With This:

Now whenever I want something I feel like I can't say it. My opinion doesn't matter and my wants and desires come secondary to everyone else. There's still no point in fighting for what I want.

Summit and Storm

I reached the ridge, my hands were raw,
Jagged stone beneath my claws.
The wind it howls, the snow it bites,
Clear skies ahead, yet darker nights.

I climbed each slope, step by step,
Every scar and cut, I've kept.
The ground gave way beneath my feet,
Avalanches knocked me off the peak.
Each summit gained, another cliff in sight,
A higher challenge, a longer fight.
My breath was frost, my limbs were numb,
The mountain's voice said, "You've just begun."
I reach for ledges, grasping thin air,
The storm reminds me you're never fair.
Every victory met with new ascent,
A path of pain that never relents.
I trace the ridge, the edges sharp,
Each jagged stone a frozen mark.
I fight the climb, my pulse a drum,
The tempest warns that it's not done.

The winds scream loud, I strain to stand,
The mountain bites with icy hands.
I see the sun, but clouds return,
Each summit reached, the cliffs still burn.

The endless climb, it never ends,
Jagged mountains, in my head.
Snow and stone, make me bleed,
Cold wind howls, need some heat.
I push, I climb, another step,
Can't stop now, never rest.
The storm is near, need to move
If I don't… I will lose…It all.

The jagged stone grinds under my hands,
The wind it whispers impossible demands.

Each step I take, the cliff ahead,
The snow it shifts, the path I dread.
I've learned to brace, to bend, to fight,
But nothing halts this endless height.
My heart pounds cold, my mind is raw,
The climb reminds me of every flaw.
I reach for air, the storm replies,
Avalanches fall from frozen skies.
The mountain tests, it never yields,
Each summit gained brings new fields.
I strain, I push, I call for aid,
But icy gusts leave me afraid.
The climb persists, relentless, grim,
Each step uncertain, each horizon dim.

I glimpse the sun above the snow,
A fleeting warmth, a fleeting glow.
But clouds descend, the winds reform,
No rest awaits — summit and storm.

The endless climb, it never ends,
Jagged mountains, in my head.
Snow and stone, make me bleed,
Cold wind howls, need some heat.
I push, I climb, another step,
Can't stop now, never rest.
The storm is near, need to move
If I don't... I will lose... It all.

Hands raw, breath thin, I stand,
Another cliff, another hand.
The mountain waits, the storm swarms,
The climb goes on — summit and storm.

Song Summary:
The Sisyphean nightmare of perpetual striving without arrival, where each summit reveals another higher peak beyond it.

What I Was Actually Writing About:
I remember the last time my father hit me. I was 15 years old and we were standing outside by the clothes line. My father had open handed slapped me across my face. I didn't cry, I didn't groan. My head twisted to the side but then my eyes returned and met his. He could see in my eyes that he would never hit me again. I don't remember having the thought of fighting back, I just remember looking at him like you're weak. From then on his abuse evolved to be more psychological than before. So I was able to escape the physical abuse, but then the emotional abuse was the next summit. The mountain represents being pushed forward into endless new challenges. I climb brutal terrain, reach what should be victory, only to discover another, higher peak beyond it. There is no summit, no completion, no moment of having finally done enough—only jagged mountains that multiply infinitely. The central exhaustion is the effort that never converts to achievement. I've climbed, I've suffered, I've paid the physical and emotional cost, yet that proximity to apparent goal only reveals its illusory nature.

The Pattern/Mechanism:
The song captures the brutal environment of these perpetual demands. Jagged stone beneath my claws, the snow it bites, the wind it howls—this isn't gentle growth or natural development but violent struggle against hostile conditions. Avalanches knocked me off the peak—even progress already made gets destroyed, forcing me to re-climb terrain I'd already conquered. Every victory met with new ascent, a path of pain that never relents—achievement brings no rest, only escalated expectations. The imagery connects directly to the father's controlling demands. Each time I met one standard, proved one capability, satisfied one requirement, a new and higher bar appeared. The mountain's voice said, "You've just begun"—there was no acknowledgment of distance traveled, only emphasis on distance remaining.

The Tension:

The physical toll mirrors emotional devastation. My hands were raw, my breath was frost, my limbs were numb, my heart pounds cold, my mind is raw—I'm being broken down by relentless demands that exceed human capacity. The desperate urgency— "Can't stop now, never rest," "need to move, if I don't... I will lose... it all"—reveals how these impossible standards were enforced through threat. Stopping meant catastrophic consequences; resting meant losing everything. I remember the last time my father hit me. I was 15 years old. My head twisted to the side but then my eyes returned and met his. He could see he would never hit me again. From then on his abuse evolved to be more psychological. So I was able to escape the physical abuse, but then the emotional abuse was the next summit.

Where I Am With This:

I catastrophize everything. I see obstacles that don't exist because I'm doomsday planning for every situation. Every time I think I'm making progress I see the next mountain I need to climb. It's exhausting.

The Poison Bloom

In the barren fields where nothing grows,
I found a bloom where the dead wind blows.
Its petals gleamed, with vivid whites,
Made me believe, it was full of life.

I reached for hope with calloused hands,
In a garden made of broken plans.
Every thorn, it whispered lies,
Dressed in silk, in thin disguise.
You smiled sweet through bitter rain,
Made me forget my years of pain.
But beauty fades and colors dry,
You can't grow truth where ashes lie.
The roots ran deep in tainted clay,
Feeding off what slipped away.
The bloom was bright, but hearts decay,
And I was blind to what it'd say.
You said love heals, but I was fooled,
A fragile heart, too easily ruled.
By poison sweet, I took my doom,
And called it love — the poison bloom.

Every petal fell too soon,
Perfumed lies beneath the moon.
I tried to hold, but could not see,
The bloom had wrapped its thorns in me.

Through all the pain in my life,
A flower, pure, gave me light.
In the wasteland, beauty lived,
I gave it all that I could give.
But poison slowly warped my mind,
Closed my eyes, and made me blind.
A fragile hope, a fatal tune,
I breathed you in — the poison bloom.

The soil cracked where trust should grow,
No rain would fall, no roots would show.

Each touch burned deep beneath my skin,
The pain I knew would start again.
I chased the sun through choking air,
Found no warmth, no comfort there.
You smiled cold, a ghostly hue,
A mirror's lie — what I thought was true.
Your thorns tore deep, I couldn't flee,
Love was the cage surrounding me.
I gave and bled until I knew,
The only bloom that grew — was you.
And in your gaze, I saw my sin,
To think a heart could heal within.
I begged for life, but met my tomb,
The grave was love — the poison bloom.

The soil was cracked, no rain to mend,
The roots reached out to find their end.
The sky went dry, the color fled,
And life forgot the tears it shed.
No growth, no sound, just dust and doom,
Where once there bloomed — the poison bloom.

Through all the pain in my life,
A flower, pure, gave me light.
In the wasteland, beauty lived,
I gave it all that I could give.
But poison slowly warped my mind,
Closed my eyes, and made me blind.
A fragile hope, a fatal tune,
I breathed you in — the poison bloom.

I had no more blood to bleed,
You took the last of what was me.
Left for dead beneath the moon,
I became the poison bloom.

Song Summary:
Becoming vulnerable to toxic relationships disguised as love after childhood devastation, where beautiful flowers were actually poison feeding on existing wounds.

What I Was Actually Writing About:
I had one primary girlfriend in high school, and then one primary girlfriend in my freshman year of college. Each one of these girls were beautiful to me. After experiencing what I endured as a kid, seeing someone who looked like they did, and saw me, I thought that was enough. I looked past all the obvious flaws and was unable to release myself from a hostile relationship. I was manipulated, demeaned, emasculated, and was not valued like an equal in the relationships. The central metaphor of a beautiful but poisonous flower captures the seductive danger. Devastated by parental abuse, these relationships appeared as miraculous hope. But what looked like salvation was actually another form of destruction. The central deception is beauty masking toxicity. I was desperate for connection and care after a childhood devoid of both, encountered relationships that presented as love but operated as exploitation. The manipulation came wrapped in affection, the harm delivered through gestures that mimicked care. I was already wounded, already exhausted, making me susceptible to anyone offering apparent tenderness.

The Pattern/Mechanism:
The song reveals how these relationships fed on my damage. Toxic partners didn't heal my wounds but exploited them, drawing sustenance from vulnerability and need. The temporary relief from suffering felt like love, the brief respite from loneliness felt like connection, but these were anesthetic effects rather than genuine care. There's self-recognition of my role in the dynamic. Childhood abuse left me with compromised ability to recognize healthy versus unhealthy relationships. Having been trained that love includes control, manipulation, and pain, I couldn't identify these elements as red flags. I poured myself into these relationships with desperate intensity, hoping to finally receive the care I'd always been denied, not recognizing I was being drained rather than nourished.

158

The Tension:

The imagery of wasteland and poison working together creates devastating portrait. In the barren fields where nothing grows—my internal landscape after childhood trauma—I found a bloom where the dead wind blows. In that devastation, anything appearing alive seemed miraculous, worth any cost. But beauty fades and colors dry, you can't grow truth where ashes lie—genuine love can't take root in the wreckage of unhealed trauma. After experiencing what I endured as a kid, seeing someone beautiful who actually saw me, I thought that was enough. I looked past all the obvious flaws and was unable to release myself from a hostile relationship.

Where I Am With This:

This might have helped me protect myself against things that are too good to be true, but it also affects me by not appreciating what I have. I'm always looking for the negativity, for what's wrong.

Is This Me?

I see the outline, pale and still,
A shape I know, yet never will.
Eyes once bright, now empty stare,
I watch myself — but I'm not there.

Drifting through a memory's frame,
A ghost that whispers my own name.
Every scar, a map, a mark,
Guides me deeper through the dark.
I used to dream, I used to try,
Now I float between alive and why.
The man I was — he's gone, decayed,
A hollow echo that time betrayed.
The past still breathes beneath my skin,
It pulls me back, drags me in.
I talk to walls, they talk to me,
In tones of shame and apathy.
I reach for warmth but find the cold,
The truth I buried has taken hold.

Can't escape the weight of me,
A shadow lost, I cease to be.
Every voice says, "You're not free,"
And I can't tell if this is me.

Am I the ghost, or the one who's dead?
Trapped in the thoughts I've always fed.
The mirror cracks, but still it shows,
The version of me that no one knows.
The air grows thick, I start to fade,
Another soul the dark has made.
I reach for light, but all I see —
Is nothing left of what was me.

Steps through dust, a faded sound,
My pulse is gone, but I'm still bound.
Every failure, carved in stone,
A graveyard built from what I've known.

The demons hum their quiet hymn,
Their song is low, their patience thin.
They wear my face, they steal my tone,
Now I speak, but not alone.
I hear them laugh when I pretend,
That pain can break, that I can mend.
Each breath I take feels undeserved,
A ghost of worth, a line unlearned.
The fog consumes, I start to fall,
A hollow man inside the wall.

I see my body, still and bare,
But there's no peace, no comfort there.
The shell remains, the soul has fled,
The man I was — already dead.

Am I the ghost, or the one who's dead?
Trapped in the thoughts I've always fed.
The mirror cracks, but still it shows,
The version of me that no one knows.
The world moves on, it doesn't see,
The hollow form I came to be.
The silence grows — no voice, no plea,
Just what's left... and it's not me.

The air is cold, the night is long,
No more right, no more wrong.
The heart's gone quiet, the mind won't see —
What's left behind was never me.

Song Summary:

The devastating existential crisis of confronting whether accumulated trauma is temporary condition or permanent identity — whether this broken version is who I actually am.

What I Was Actually Writing About:

My family and my romantic relationships had deteriorated, those I thought were my friends made moves on my girlfriends, so I thought this is just who I am. I believed that this was all there was for me. This abusive cycle of relationships that were always less than ideal. After cataloging abuse, toxic relationships, and emotional numbness, I arrive at the terrifying question: is this who I actually am? Not who I've temporarily become due to circumstances, but my fundamental, unchangeable nature? The central horror is the potential collapse of distinction between damaged self and authentic self. I look at myself and see something simultaneously familiar and alien, unable to recognize whether this traumatized, defended, struggling person is the real me or a distortion created by abuse.

The Pattern/Mechanism:

The song traces the loss of the person I used to be — or might have been. I used to dream, I used to try, now I float between alive and why — agency, aspiration, vitality have all eroded. The man I was — he's gone, decayed, a hollow echo that time betrayed. There's mourning for a self that may never have fully existed, a potential person destroyed before they could develop. The question becomes whether that lost person was ever real or just an illusion, whether my current traumatized state is aberration or truth. The imagery of haunting and ghosts pervades. Drifting through a memory's frame, a ghost that whispers my own name — I exist in liminal space between presence and absence, neither fully alive nor completely gone. I talk to walls, they talk to me, in tones of shame and apathy — isolation has progressed to the point where internal voices have replaced human connection, and those voices speak only criticism and emptiness.

The Tension:

The refrain "Am I the ghost, or the one who's dead?" captures the fundamental confusion about what remains. Has trauma killed some

162

essential part, leaving only a haunting shadow? Or am I the ghost, and what I'm mourning is an idealized self that never actually existed? Trapped in the thoughts I've always fed—I recognize my role in sustaining these patterns but can't determine if the thoughts define me or distort me. The demons hum their quiet hymn, their song is low, their patience thin. They wear my face, they steal my tone, now I speak, but not alone—the buried demons have merged with my identity so completely that separation seems impossible. My family and my romantic relationships had deteriorated, those I thought were my friends made moves on my girlfriends, so I thought this is just who I am.

Where I Am With This:

This is still a prevalent feeling in my day to day life. Am I destined to encounter all these obstacles? Every trauma, every abuse, has tainted my lens to perceive the worst things, even when good things surround me.

Run Free

The gates were tall, the air was still,
The night was sharp, the world could kill.
But through the dark, I found my key,
The chains fell off — I ran free.

Bars of guilt, walls of pain,
Echoes whisper my old name.
Every step a ghost behind,
Every breath a threat in kind.
The beasts still howl, their teeth still bare,
But I'm not theirs, I'm not there.
I bled for years in someone's game,
I broke the mold, I shed the shame.
The moon was pale, the field was wide,
I ran with fear right by my side.
But fear grew tired, I kept the pace,
And found myself in open space.
No collar left, no voice commands,
I own my soul, I use my hands.
No master's eyes to weigh my worth,
I found my place upon this earth.

The beasts still roar, but fade away,
Their echoes die with the break of day.
I see the light, I start to see —
I'm finally who I'm meant to be.

I ran through fire, I ran through stone,
I learned that freedom stands alone.
The past still calls, but can't reach me,
I buried the pain, I let it be.
My chains are gone, my heart beats true,
I found my peace in something new.
No blood required, no legacy —
My family found, they chose me.

No more begging for a name,
No more bending under blame.

The road ahead is rough, it bends,
But now I walk beside my friends.
No looking back, no glance behind,
No ghosts left crawling through my mind.
The cell I built, I left unlocked,
The doors all open, the fear all stopped.
I carved my worth from shattered bones,
Made my voice from broken tones.
The world once dark, now glows with hue,
A brighter sky, a clearer view.
Not bound by blood, but by belief,
The ones I found — they gave me peace.
The storm still stirs, the night still calls,
But I walk tall beyond those walls.

The beasts may chase, but I won't hide,
Their growls now fade against the tide.
I've seen the light, I've paid the fee,
The gates are gone — I'm finally free.

I ran through fire, I ran through stone,
I learned that freedom stands alone.
The past still calls, but can't reach me,
I buried the pain, I let it be.
My chains are gone, my heart beats true,
I found my peace in something new.
No blood required, no legacy —
My family found, they chose me.

The night is still, the stars align,
I leave the dark I called mine.
No beasts, no gates, no memory —
Just quiet steps... and I am free.

Song Summary:
The pivotal moment of physical escape through military service, breaking chains and discovering self-ownership for the first time.

What I Was Actually Writing About:
I joined the military. I escaped my home town. I feel like my small town in Wisconsin was a prison that confined me. People didn't leave, they just got older. A cycle of purgatory. So when I joined the military and was able to leave, I broke free from those chains. I was married to the girlfriend from college. It took a long time to be fully free of the past, but this was the catalyst for being more emotionally free than I had ever been before. Military service provided what nothing else could: legitimate escape from the family system, distance from the town that held all my trauma, and entry into a structured world where I could begin discovering who I might become outside the definitions imposed by abuse. The central experience is the exhilaration of breaking chains. The escape wasn't safe or easy, but it was possible. I seized the opportunity, understanding that remaining meant continued suffocation. The prison was both literal—the family home, the controlling father— and psychological—internalized shame and damage. But in this moment, I chose flight.

The Pattern/Mechanism:
The song acknowledges that escape doesn't erase trauma. The beasts still howl, their teeth still bare, but I'm not theirs, I'm not there—the demons, the internalized abuse, the damage all persist. Every step a ghost behind, every breath a threat in kind—I run while still carrying the psychological weight of everything documented in previous songs. But crucially, there's new physical distance: I'm not theirs, I'm not there. The father can't control from across the country. The mother's denial doesn't reach into this new space. The toxic relationships exist in the past rather than the present. The imagery of running captures both flight and freedom. The moon was pale, the field was wide, I ran with fear right by my side—this wasn't confident striding into a secure future but desperate flight from untenable past, fear accompanying every step.

166

The Tension:

The most powerful element is the discovery of self-ownership. I own my soul, I use my hands—perhaps for the first time, my life belongs to me rather than being controlled by others. No collar left, no voice commands—the Marionette's strings are cut, the quicksand left behind, the mountain abandoned. No master's eyes to weigh my worth, I found my place upon this earth—worth is no longer determined by the father's impossible standards or measured against perpetually moving goalposts. I can simply exist without constant evaluation and judgment. I joined the military. I escaped my home town. I feel like my small town in Wisconsin was a prison that confined me. When I joined the military and was able to leave, I broke free from those chains.

Where I Am With This:

This might explain why I've job hopped so much. When I was able to get away from childhood abuse I did it by removing myself from the situation. Now whenever my walls close in, my first reaction is to leave. I'm always running.

Whispers Return

I thought I buried all my fears,
Laid them down through all those years.
But silence breaks — it calls my name,
Familiar voices, back again.

They crawl from cracks in the floor I sealed,
The ghosts I fought, the wounds I healed.
I turn the key, but the lock won't hold,
The whisper's warm, the breath is cold.
I tell myself, "That's not my mind,"
But they twist the truth, they blur the line.
Every doubt I've drowned before,
Comes knocking now, demanding more.
I hear my name in empty halls,
The sound rebounds, the courage falls.
The calm I built begins to shake,
The ground gives way, the fears awake.

I close my eyes, I count to ten,
The noise fades out, then starts again.
They say I'm nothing, again and again,
They say the dark will always win…

But I've got hands that pull me through,
Voices stronger, pure and true.
The storm may scream, the night may spin,
But I won't let the dark back in.
You stood by me when I broke down,
Your light still burns when mine burns out.
I won't run — I'll stand, begin,
To fight the dark, not let it win.

They whisper sweet like they used to sing,
They say I'll fall — the same old thing.
But I've seen fire, I've seen the flood,
I've bled enough to know my blood.
They show me mirrors, cracked and bent,
The faces there are years I've spent.

But every scar, each line I've worn,
Is proof I've lived, not just been torn.
I hear the storm, I feel it near,
The thunder hums inside my ear.
The air grows thick, the shadows grin,
But this time I don't cave in.

The wind still howls, but I stand tall,
I've learned the art of not to fall.
They whisper close, they press my skin,
But I'm not who I've ever been.

I've got hands that pull me through,
Voices stronger, pure and true.
The beasts return, the dark creeps in,
But love reminds me where I've been.
You held me up, you brought me light,
Through endless storms, through sleepless nights.
I won't fade — I'll rise again,
The light remains, the dark won't win.

The whispers fade, they lose their spin,
I found my strength — and those within.
Faint echoes linger, soft and thin,
The dark survives, but it won't win.

Song Summary:
The harsh reality that physical distance doesn't eliminate internalized trauma—the demons traveled with me despite geographic escape.

What I Was Actually Writing About:
Even though I got out of my hometown, things progressed, I was still haunted by my past. When writing these songs I also brought up some of those old feelings that I had repressed, even though some of my emotional ticks were a result of them. I could feel them coming back to life, feel those emotions and understand why I act the way I act. It's acknowledging the fact that these emotions still exist, even when I tried to suppress them. Geography changed, but the psychological architecture built during years of abuse remains intact, and the voices that were suppressed during the excitement of liberation begin demanding attention again. The central devastating recognition is that burial wasn't elimination. I believed that leaving home, joining the military, finding chosen family had resolved the trauma. The demons aren't external forces left behind in the hometown; they're internalized presences, revealing that suppression was always temporary containment rather than permanent solution.

The Pattern/Mechanism:
The song captures the horror of recognizing patterns I thought I'd escaped. My defenses, which seemed solid in the new environment, prove inadequate against the returning voices. Every doubt I've drowned before, comes knocking now, demanding more. The escape provided respite, but the fundamental wounds remain unhealed, and the coping mechanisms that helped me survive the abusive home resurface in the new context. The imagery emphasizes invasive persistence. They crawl from cracks, I hear my name in empty halls, the noise fades out, then starts again—the demons are patient, waiting for moments of vulnerability, exploiting quiet when my guard drops. The specific content of the whispers connects to everything documented before. They say I'm nothing, again and again, they say the dark will always win—these aren't new messages but the internalized voice of the abusive father, the controlling

170

standards, the toxic relationships, all speaking through my own thoughts.

The Tension:

However, this song introduces a crucial new element: resistance supported by connection. But I've got hands that pull me through, voices stronger, pure and true—the chosen family from "Run Free" provides counterweight to the demons. You stood by me when I broke down, your light still burns when mine burns out. Unlike the mother who abandoned ("The Fallen Beacon"), these people stay present during struggle. The refrain shifts from passive suffering to active defiance: But I won't let the dark back in—this is declaration of intent, recognition that the whispers return but don't have to dominate. Even though I got out of my hometown, things progressed, I was still haunted by my past. When writing these songs I brought up some of those old feelings that I had repressed.

Where I Am With This:

This is about my writing process. By writing these feelings down, they both returned but also feel somewhat controlled, at least my past demons. The effects are still alive and real. They don't control me as much as they used to.

Control

The halls are quiet, cold, and deep,
My monsters stir, but they don't creep.
Their whispers fade to distant hum,
They know who's master — what I've become.

I built these walls from fractured thought,
Stone by stone, from fights I fought.
Each cell a name, each lock a sin,
Each voice that once lived deep within.
They claw, they beg, they hiss my name,
But fear now bends beneath my flame.
They used to bite, they used to bleed,
Now they starve unless I feed.
The keys hang heavy in my hand,
Their cries still echo through the land.
I walk the halls — my kingdom, mine,
A grave reborn by my design.
Their laughter dull, their hunger low,
They pace and wait — but I say no.

I give them time, I give them breath,
A sip of pain, a taste of death.
But when they scream, I turn the key —
And let them know they live for me.

I hold the door, I own the key,
The ghosts still live, but serve to me.
Their claws once sharp now scratch the floor,
They howl, but they can't reach the door.
The dark still hums, it tries to rise,
But I'm the storm behind their eyes.
They breathe my air, they move, they see —
But only when I set them free.

They snarl in rhythm, hum in tune,
A choir cursed beneath the moon.
Each voice a past I can't erase,
But now I choose which one I face.

The liar whispers, "Let me out,"
The fear still trembles, full of doubt.
The anger hums its steady song,
But I decide if it stays long.
They used to rule, they used to reign,
Now they exist within my brain.
A mental prison of my design,
Locked away for all of time.
I feed them crumbs, they snarl, they eat,
I tap the bars and keep the beat.
The keys still jingle, soft, serene,
A lullaby for what I've been.

They're part of me, I can't deny,
The parts that lived, the ones that die.
But I decide how loud they scream —
I own the dark, I own the dream.

I hold the door, I own the key,
The ghosts still live, but serve to me.
The echoes fade, the night grows still,
I feed their hunger when I will.
They bow their heads, they know their place,
The bars reflect my hardened face.
The dark still hums — it always will,
But now it hums beneath my will.

The keys still shine, they hum, they gleam,
The locks all hum my final theme.
They live below, they pace, they plea —
But now the warden's finally me.

Song Summary:
Achieving dominance over demons through transformation from victim of internal voices to warden of internal prison, managing rather than eliminating trauma.

What I Was Actually Writing About:
By writing these down, by turning them into lyrics, I'm able to capture them in a moment in time and transform them. These emotions still exist, but it's a form of therapy by journaling how I feel. I can't truly control my feelings and emotions, but when I feel sad, or angry, I take those feelings and I write a poem, I write lyrics, and I turn them into art. I try to tell a story about why I feel the way I feel, find some sort of resolution, and manage my emotions the best that I can. I know I can't truly heal, but I can manage. The central achievement is the power reversal. The demons remain active presences, but their movement is constrained. I've established hierarchy where I command and the demons obey, or at least remain contained. This internal architecture was constructed through conscious effort, each battle with the demons providing material for their eventual containment. The imagery of prison with me as warden inverts the earlier metaphors. In "Marionette," I was imprisoned by the father's control. In "The Quicksand Wins," I was trapped by circumstances. Now I've imprisoned the forces that once imprisoned me.

The Pattern/Mechanism:
The song reveals this isn't peaceful coexistence but controlled hostility. They claw, they beg, they hiss my name, but fear now bends beneath my flame—the demons still want dominance, still attempt manipulation, but I've become stronger than they are. They used to bite, they used to bleed, now they starve unless I feed—the demons no longer have independent access to my emotional life. They exist only insofar as I permit, sustained by controlled rations rather than feeding freely on fear and pain. The refrain "I hold the door, I own the key" emphasizes absolute authority. The ghosts still live, but serve to me—acknowledgment that the demons are permanent but subordinate. The dark still hums—it always will, but now it hums beneath my will.

The Tension:

There's complex acknowledgment of integration. They're part of me, I can't deny, the parts that lived, the ones that die — the demons aren't foreign invaders but aspects of self, responses to trauma, survival mechanisms that became destructive. But I decide how loud they scream — I own the dark, I own the dream. I accept these damaged parts as belonging to my psyche while refusing to be defined or controlled by them. This represents mature trauma processing: not denial, not identification, but integration. By writing these down, by turning them into lyrics, I'm able to capture them in a moment in time and transform them. I can't truly control my feelings and emotions, but when I feel sad, or angry, I take those feelings and I write. I know I can't truly heal, but I can manage.

Where I Am With This:

This is me controlling my demons by putting them in lyrics. Giving them the voice they need but not allowing them to dictate like they used to. When I'm feeling bad, I write those feelings down and capture them. It allows me to express myself and gain relief.

Afterword:
Giving Voice to the Buried

These aren't just poems. They were always meant to be more than words on a page.

When I started writing these, I didn't know what I was doing. I just knew I needed to get something out—something that had been buried so deep I'd almost convinced myself it wasn't there anymore. But it was there. It's always been there. And keeping it locked inside wasn't protecting me anymore. It was suffocating me.

What Writing This Has Done For Me

I found that journaling helped. Putting this stuff down gave me the space to say things I had held inside for so long, to poetically discuss difficult topics that would be too raw in plain language. There's something about shaping pain into verse, about finding rhythm in chaos, that creates just enough distance to look at it without drowning in it.

Writing these songs became my therapy. When I feel sad, angry, affected by my past, I find myself writing. I can write a song in about an hour and get that relief very quickly. I find a way to express it, process it, get it down, and it has a space. Its own prison cell.

Every song was an exhumation. Digging up what I'd buried, what I'd tried to forget, what I'd pretended didn't matter. The demons I documented in Collection III—I spent decades trying to keep them locked inside. Writing them down meant opening those doors, letting them out, looking directly at what I'd been avoiding. And then containing them again, but this time on my terms. In words I chose. In forms I controlled.

It's been psychologically necessary. Trauma creates fragmentation. Different parts of you hold different memories, different responses, different ages of pain. Writing these songs was integration work. The part of me that still believes in beauty, that still shows up, that still tries—that part got to speak. The part that knows what survival costs, that carries the weight, that refuses to pretend—that part got to speak too. And they got to speak in the same song, at the same time, without one having to silence the other.

The demons still live in the halls. But I wrote the architecture. I gave them names. I documented their origins. I described their effects. And in doing that, I claimed authority over them. Not control—I'll never have complete control. But authority. The right to say: this is what you are, this is what you did to me, and this is how I'm choosing to carry you now.

Why I Made Them Songs

For myself, I needed to hear my pain in someone else's voice. Even an AI's voice. Because when it's only in my head, I can dismiss it. I can minimize it. I can tell myself I'm exaggerating. I can tell myself it doesn't matter, but when I hear it performed—when the words refuse to let me pretend it's not that bad—I can't deny it anymore. The pain becomes real because it's externalized. Hearing someone else—something else—deliver my words made me feel like I'm not alone, like I'm seen.

Some may ask why I published these songs, why not just listen to them on my own? That answer is simple. If someone else is experiencing the same pain as me, my words may give them hope that they're not alone, that they have someone else who knows how they feel. It may sound cliché, but if I can save someone who may think of self-harm, I want to. I want to try. And if that sounds cliché or like a lie, so be it—it's true to me.

Because someone out there is carrying the same weight I carried. Maybe they don't read poetry. Maybe they can't articulate what they're feeling. But maybe they'll hear a song—in their car, while doing dishes and something will crack open inside of them. They'll hear themselves in these words. And they'll know: this is what trauma sounds like. If you hear yourself in this, you're not uniquely broken. This is documented experience.

About the Music

I chose orchestral rap because that contrast—that deliberate, jarring dissonance—is what trauma feels like to me. The orchestra is what people see: the composed surface, the performance of normalcy. The rap is what you carry: the hypervigilance, the catastrophic thoughts, the brutal honesty you can't voice in polite conversation. When they collide, when beauty and brutality exist in the same measure, that's the authenticity I was chasing. Because that's what it's actually like to live with severe trauma. You're functional and drowning. You're achieving and barely surviving.

I need to give credit where it's due: NF's music showed me what was possible. Hearing his songs—the raw emotion, the vulnerability, the refusal to make pain palatable—inspired me to pursue this genre. The way he delivers brutal honesty over cinematic production, the way he lets the music swell while the words cut deep, the way he doesn't apologize for the weight he carries. That resonated with me. His music proved that trauma could be art without being sanitized. But I also knew mine needed to be different. Mine needed to capture my truth, my contradictions, my particular flavor of survival.

The AI didn't write these songs—I did. Every word is mine. Every emotion is mine. Every demon documented is mine. The AI gave them voice. But the voice speaks my truth, in the form I chose, with the contrast I needed to make that truth visible.

The Journey Through These Collections

These three collections form a comprehensive narrative of my trauma's origin, the manifestation inside of me, and my management—a brutal but honest documentation of how my childhood abuse shaped every aspect of my human existence.

Collection I: What I Feel Inside operates as the surface layer, documenting symptoms without fully understanding their source. I struggle with trust, hypervigilance, emotional regulation, and relationship dysfunction. I could describe what was wrong—the inability to open up, the constant planning that stole joy, the silent expectations and subsequent doubt when needs were voiced, the fear of abandonment, the apathy that protected against feeling. But these were presented as isolated struggles, personality flaws, or unfortunate patterns rather than as coherent responses to specific trauma. The collection ended with tentative reach toward connection, suggesting that shared vulnerability might offer healing.

Collection II: Weight of Me shifted perspective from seeking connection to claiming solitary strength. I revealed how I carry invisible suffering while appearing functional, how achievements go unrecognized, how I see my despised father in myself, how I perpetually search for purpose and belonging without finding either. The questioning, the overthinking, the exhaustion—all documented with weary defiance. This collection ended not with reaching toward others but with fierce declaration of self-sufficiency: the pain has been training, the survival itself is victory, and I'm prepared for whatever comes next.

Collection III: My Demons descended beneath both previous collections to excavate the source. Here, finally, I named what created all the patterns documented before: a father who terrorized through explosive violence, impossible standards, total control, and punishment for any resistance; a mother who abandoned me to abuse and later denied it occurred; toxic romantic relationships that exploited vulnerabilities created by family trauma; and the resulting question of whether any authentic self survived this onslaught. The collection charts escape through military service, the discovery that physical distance doesn't eliminate internalized demons, and eventual transformation from victim of internal voices to warden of them—achieving not healing but management, not peace but control.

What I Hope You Take From This

If you're a trauma survivor reading this, or listening to my music, I hope you find validation in seeing your experience documented. The part of you that shows up for work, that smiles at appropriate moments, that tries so hard to be normal. That's real. The part of you that's drowning underneath, that can't stop cataloging danger, that's exhausted from the performance. That's real too. Both exist. The contradiction is the truth.

If you're creating something from your pain—writing, art, music, anything—I hope this gives you permission to let it be contradictory. To refuse to make it neat. To let beauty and brutality coexist without resolving the tension. Trauma isn't clean. Art about trauma shouldn't be either.

If you're struggling to articulate what you're experiencing, maybe these songs give you language. Maybe the genre itself becomes metaphor: I'm orchestral rap. I'm the collision between what you see and what I carry.

The Question of Resolution

The collections refuse easy redemption narratives. I don't:

- Forgive my abusers
- Fully heal from my trauma
- Achieve stable happiness
- Form effortlessly trusting relationships
- Eliminate the demons
- Transcend my past

Instead, I:

- Survive, repeatedly, despite circumstances designed to break me
- Name the specific abuse and its specific effects
- Escape the immediate danger through military service
- Find chosen family who provide different relationship models
- Learn to manage rather than be managed by internalized trauma
- Claim authority over my internal landscape

This represents honest rather than hopeful conclusion. Some trauma—particularly severe, prolonged childhood abuse—creates permanent alteration. The person I might have been without trauma never got to exist. The question isn't "how do I return to who I was before?" but "how do I build a life with the person trauma made me?"

The collections answer: through naming, through escape when possible, through connection when bearable, through management when healing isn't available, and through sheer determined refusal to let the demons have complete victory.

Final Words

Writing this book hasn't healed me. But it's helped me. It gave me a process—a way to take what's chaotic and suffocating inside and give it shape, give it form, give it a cell where it can exist without consuming me.

If there's a unifying thread across all three collections, it's my absolute refusal to surrender. I was dealt catastrophic damage in the most vulnerable period of development by the very people meant to protect me. I've struggled with trust, emotional regulation, identity, purpose, and connection in ways that make simply continuing to exist a daily achievement. I've contemplated whether any authentic self survived the trauma. I've run from demons only to discover the demons traveled with me.

And yet.

I'm still here. Still fighting. Still refusing to let the abuse have complete victory.

I become, ultimately, what I needed in childhood: a fierce protector who refuses to abandon, who maintains boundaries against harm, who says "no more" to forces that would control or destroy. I perform this role for myself, internally, adult self protecting child parts that still carry the terror of the house of wrath.

This is triumph of a specific kind—not over trauma but within traumatized existence. The demons live in the halls; they always will. The scars remain; they've shaped the very structure of self. But I hold the keys, I make the decisions, I own my life in ways that seemed impossible when I was the child running through the yard, hoping his storm would pass me by.

These collections don't offer hope in the conventional sense—no promise that everything will be fine, that healing is inevitable, that trauma's effects can be transcended. Instead, they offer something perhaps more valuable: testimony that survival is possible, that management is achievable, that you can build a life even when the foundation is cracked, that the demons can be controlled even when they can't be defeated.

For those who carry similar weight, who fight similar demons, who question whether they'll ever feel safe or whole or capable of genuine connection—these collections say: You're not alone in this. The struggle you face is real, not imagined. The effects you experience are predictable responses to terrible circumstances, not personal failures. And while the path forward may not lead to complete healing, it can lead somewhere better than where you've been.

I stand at the end, scarred and exhausted, holding keys to internal prison where demons pace and whisper. It's not the ending anyone would choose. But it's an ending claimed through fierce determination, hard-won understanding, and absolute refusal to let trauma write the final chapter.

The warden is finally me. The keys are finally mine. The demons are locked inside. The life, however difficult, is finally my own.

And sometimes, after everything, that's enough.

Where to Listen

You can hear the music across all major platforms under the artist name **LockedInside**. I have several albums available, but this book draws from only three of them: the three that cut the deepest and reveal the most honest version of who I am.

Thank you.

www.ingramcontent.com/pod-product-compliance
Lightning Source LLC
Chambersburg PA
CBHW072019060426
42446CB00044B/2804